Hailed as the Inter~~~~~~~~~~~ award-winning blogger and YouTuber w~~~~~ million total views to date. She is also a BBC docume~~~~~ presenter and summer 2016 saw her debut the hit documentary 'Clean Eating's Dirty Secrets'. Additionally, Grace is also a dedicated body-image campaigner, has presented London Fashion Week and has worked with brands including L'Oréal, Clinique, ASOS and New Look, to name but a few.

GRACE VICTORY
NO FILTER

HEADLINE

First published in Great Britain in 2017
by HEADLINE PUBLISHING GROUP

First published in paperback in 2018
by HEADLINE PUBLISHING GROUP

1

Cataloguing in Publication Data is available from the British Library

Paperback ISBN 978 1 4722 4772 8

Typeset in 11.25/14.8 pt Source Sans Pro by Jouve (UK), Milton Keynes

Printed and bound in Great Britain by Clays Ltd, Elcograf S.p.A.

While everything in this book is true some names have been changed.

The information contained in this book is not intended to replace the services
of trained medical professionals or to be a substitute for medical advice.
You are advised to consult a doctor on any matters relating to your health,
and in particular on any matters that may require diagnosis or medical attention.

Headline's policy is to use papers that are natural, renewable and
recyclable products and made from wood grown in sustainable forests.
The logging and manufacturing processes are expected to conform to the
environmental regulations of the country of origin.

HEADLINE PUBLISHING GROUP
An Hachette UK Company
Carmelite House
50 Victoria Embankment
London EC4Y 0DZ

www.headline.co.uk
www.hachette.co.uk

For any woman who needs a reason NOT to give up. This is it.

CONTENTS

Prologue

'I want to die.'

I stared at the words I had scratched into the grey school desk moments before. The scraggy, erratic letters stared back at me. Not a question, but a statement. Being alive was hurting too much and I wasn't sure I could take much more of it.

Picking up the compass again, I looked round to check no one else in my maths class was watching me. I was at the back, and could see a studious few people paying attention at the front, but everyone else was involved in their own distractions, or doing their make-up, causing chaos for the poor teacher.

I scratched deep into the grey surface again: 'I hate myself.'

The words repeated themselves inside my brain, over and over. Sadly it was true and it was one of the reasons for the tight, knotted ball that had become a permanent feature in the pit of my stomach over the last three years.

I was twelve years old, and on the surface life looked like it was pretty good for me. I was doing OK at school, had friends, a mum who loved me, and I got to spend lots of time on my favourite hobbies – dancing and acting. In fact, that side of my life was going so well for me I had even starred in a few TV shows and films, incredibly even managing to get a role in *Harry Potter*. I should have been over the moon.

But it didn't change things. On a daily basis, I hated myself and my life. I was scared, anxious, cried all the time, and didn't like how I looked or how I felt. I was fat, wore glasses, and I didn't feel like I fitted in or did anything right. If I needed proof of it, I got it when I spent a year being tormented at the hands of the school bullies. Most importantly, I thought I was never good enough for myself, or anyone else.

I knew that being an adolescent was supposed to be filled with all sorts of trauma (thanks, hormones!), but this felt like more, it felt deeper, darker. Worse than anything, I really, really hated myself.

Looking back at that scene now breaks my heart. I want to go in there, scoop that girl up, and tell her all the things I know now that might have got her through it and made things easier. I know now that I was dealing with mental health problems back then and was depressed, that I was suffering from the effects of a fucked-up childhood, a dad who was either absent or violent, body image issues and an eating disorder, just to mention a few of my problems.

But I didn't know it at the time, and instead I still had another nine years of self-loathing and self-destructive behaviour to get through before life hit its lowest point and I began to turn things around and move away from those dark places.

Therapy, good friends and retraining my way of thinking were key to the journey of self-discovery that followed. I learnt about myself, about the pressures that had been put on me by society as well as the impact my childhood, family and friends had on me.

Each time I learnt a little something more about myself, or gained a new coping mechanism, I would see it as a one brick added to building myself up. Over time, I have slowly taken all those bricks and turned them into walls, beginning to build my self-belief, self-esteem and understanding of my value. Along the way some of those walls were practically annihilated when the dark times crept back in and I felt like I was almost back to square one. But I had seen that it was possible to work my way through it, so each time I have picked myself up, dusted myself down, and said to myself, 'Come on, Grace, you can do this. You are better than that.'

At the same time I was learning how much of self-discovery comes from sharing experiences, ideas and emotions with other people. I began a job when I was twenty-one where I learnt how to tackle the problems faced by young people – and then my YouTube channel, 'Ugly Face of Beauty', happened.

Early on in my vlogging career I realised that talking about fashion and beauty wasn't going to be enough for me, and like so many others on the internet, I had been guilty of putting a sheen of perfection over my life, but my reality was far from perfect. Yes, social media, I love you, but I am looking at you as a big part of this perceived perfection problem as you make it so easy for people to pretend to be something they are not.

Instead I wanted to be honest and really talk about what I was going through. Those closest to me thought this was a bad idea, that I was leaving myself open to judgement, but I didn't want to filter out my truth any more; I wanted to be honest.

So, as terrified as I was to lay myself so bare, I made my video 'The Pressure to Be Perfect', which went online in June 2012. In it, I admitted to having suffered from depression, anxiety and self-harm. I told my viewers about my insecurities and fears, but I also told them my hopes for recovery.

And wow, the response! If there was ever a sign to me that people were desperate for some open dialogue and a role model who was less than perfect, this was it. So from then on I opened up, not necessarily admitting to everything – you will learn a lot more about my background and troubles in this book – but showing enough of myself to give people someone to relate to, letting them know that if they were going through the same thing, they were not alone.

I quickly learnt that there is power and strength in showing vulnerability, and realised that through talking about my struggles, the possibilities of helping others through theirs are endless.

I also started talking about other difficult topics and breaking down taboos, sometimes in a serious way, and other times in a more light-hearted, fun way. 'Outfit of the Day: I'm Fat, I Should Wear Bin Bags', anyone? As I have always been very open-minded anyway, talking about subjects that might be off-limits to others came naturally to me. It was as though I had found my purpose in life.

In amongst it all though, the most amazing thing happened. Although my main aim was to help others, the more I talked about my issues, the more it actually helped me. I no longer felt so alone, and I realised sharing my story was helping me become mentally stronger and happier too. Let's face it, in this messed up ol' world that we are living in right now, we all need to have each other's backs, and help a girl out. Support and empowerment is key.

All of this had such an impact on me that one morning I woke up and realised I felt like a different person. I was twenty-six years old and for the first time ever I could say that I actually did love myself. I felt lighter, more positive, as though I was capable of anything, and I no longer needed to beat myself up for who I was.

It was a long journey to reach that point. It didn't happen with just one event, or any change to my core self; it was a gradual development over time. That one particular day as I lay in bed feeling calm and secure, I knew I really did now love me, Grace Victory. And wow, what would I give to have let that twelve-year-old girl, sitting there with her compass and self-loathing, know the way that life was going to be.

I wish I could have told her that it didn't matter if I weighed more than I wanted to – because incredibly I was going to be asked to model for Nike; that school bullies mean nothing when you are older, and instead I would be connected with millions of great people online; that despite all the issues I might have with confidence, one day I was going to end up presenting for the BBC. It sounds so amazing when I put it like that!

Growing up I didn't have someone to tell me 'it's gonna be OK'. So this is my chance to try and say that to anyone who might need to hear it. This book, I hope, will be of lasting value, an infinite piece of hope and inspiration that you can flick back to when all you want to do is give up.

It hasn't been easy going back over some of the memories but if I had to go through those extremely tough times in life in order to help others, then it was more than worth it. I took on the role of the internet's big sister, and this book is an extension of that. It is great to have the space to expand on topics I have briefly touched on in my blogs and videos, as well as talking about new areas.

My key message to people is really that defying statistics and changing your life is possible – but it starts with you. With every painful experience comes a chance to grow. A chance to be the person you were always meant to be.

I think we'd all like to raise our daughters – and equally our sons – in a world where they can just be themselves. A world where they are safe, loved and empowered – something that I so desperately needed when I was growing up. I hope *No Filter* will make you cry in one chapter but laugh in the next – a true representation of my life.

I always tell people: 'Trust your journey, as every point of your life is going to help you get to where you need to be.' Here is the story of mine.

Chapter 1
HOW IT ALL BEGAN

'You can spend a lifetime trying to forget a few
minutes of your childhood.'

Everyone always says you follow in your parents' foot-
steps. Well, if I had, I would probably be living in fear of a
violent boyfriend while protecting my two kids. So I guess
you can tell I have followed my own path. My parents did, of
course, play their role in my development, though. Let's face it,
everyone's character is formed in their childhood, so anything
your mum and dad do affects the kind of person you will turn out
to be. I know mine hugely shaped me into who I am today, in
ways that are both good and bad. So if you are to understand
me – and I really hope you do by the end of this book – I need to
give you some idea of what it was like to be me growing up.

But wow, my childhood . . . You better get ready for this! You
know when you watch *EastEnders* or *Jeremy Kyle* and think 'no
way can all of that messed-up stuff happen to just one person in
real life'? Well, I can tell you it does. Domestic Violence? Check.
Kidnapping? Check. Crime? Check. And that is just scratching
the surface . . .

My first memory is a very early one, and although it is clear as day, I didn't understand the significance of it at the time. I was standing up in my cot, and holding on to the bars that ran around the edge. I was staring, confused, at the strange man in my room who was telling me: 'Shh, everything is going to be OK.'

Years later I asked Mum about it, and found out the police had raided our home looking for my dad in connection with a robbery, although he was never charged with it. It was this man's job to ensure I wasn't frightened by it. By the time I learnt this, I wasn't surprised to hear the story, and just nodded, stored the information, and got on with whatever I was doing.

I was born on 29 August 1990 to my mum Dawn, who was just twenty-one at the time. She was working in a clothes shop called Chelsea Girl when she was pregnant, but gave that up to raise me. My dad is a guy mum had known from when she was at school. He was five years older than her and one of five brothers, and all them were dating mum and her friends on and off over the years. My parents never got married and my dad never actually properly lived with us, but just drifted in and out of our lives when it suited him, appearing in some of my childhood memories, but absent from most of them.

I was brought up on a council estate in High Wycombe, in Buckinghamshire. 'Ooh,' I hear you say. 'Bucks, as in part of the posh Home Counties area? Very nice!' Uh-uh. Far from it.

High Wycombe is about thirty miles from the centre of London, and has that weird chippy vibe to it that loads of towns round the edge of the capital seem to have. It is pretty industrial, although proud of it, as you can tell by the fact there is a museum in the centre focused on the history of local chair-making. If that isn't a reason to visit, I don't know what is!

There is a lot of deprivation, and it has its fair share of crime, sadly in particular child sexual exploitation. It is also pretty dirty – apparently the fourth dirtiest place in the South East, according to a government survey when I was a teenager #factoftheday

The home I was brought up in for the first fifteen years of my life was a two-bed flat on the first floor of a three-storey block. A few of the blocks were all clumped together, forming a mini estate. It was a very concrete-looking block with communal stairwells and graffiti up the walls. Mum did her best to keep our actual flat nice though, and I was allowed to decorate my room the way I wanted. It was Noddy-themed when I was very young, then Winnie the Pooh, and then when I was eleven, half of it was pink and half purple with a border dividing it. It was proper cool at the time; I loved it!

My dad's family is from Saint Vincent, and he is black, and my mum is white. To them, that didn't seem to matter. To their families, it was another story.

Mum's family were hugely against her getting together with a black man, and when they began dating it caused all sorts of arguments. So you can imagine what it was like when she got pregnant with me . . . Apparently World War Three nearly broke out.

If you tried to draw up my family tree, there would be lines crisscrossing all over the place. Take one of my dad's brothers, for example. This uncle has six kids by four women, and kind of bounced between the women at different points in life. One of them lived above us with her two kids, and they are great, but it was sad to see them in that situation, even if it did just seem normal to me at the time.

When I was little I looked exactly like a mini version of how I do now. I haven't changed! I had massive curly hair, although my skin was a lot darker than I am now – as I got older I got paler (which pisses me off as I am always wanting a golden glow).

Until I was five, it was just my mum and me, a little team, with Dad popping in from time to time. I imagine he and Mum must still have had a relationship of sorts, as then my sister Charlotte was born. Apparently I was less than impressed by her arrival and began playing up, even throwing an egg across a café and hitting a wall in protest! Another time I got told off so I threw all my toys out of the window. Mum had to go outside and pick up every single one, and was furious about it. She told me I couldn't go outside and play and I remember stamping my feet and shouting.

I guess I was jealous that I was no longer centre of my mum's attention. It didn't help that all the uncles were nicer to Charlotte than me because of her appearance. She was the absolute spit of my nan – Dad's mum – and although my dad and his brothers had a pretty violent upbringing at the hands of their father, they all doted on their mum.

So as my sister looked like my nan, she was automatically the favourite.

Our flat had just the two bedrooms, so Charlotte and I were supposed to share, but actually that never really happened, as she just slept in with Mum. We were very different from the off. Charlotte relied very heavily on Mum, whereas I have always been independent. In some ways after she came along it felt like it was always her and Mum together, and me on the outside. I'm not sure if they would say the same, but that is how it felt to me at times.

Around this time Dad would turn up every two weeks or so, and sit on the sofa smoking weed with his brothers or friends, demanding that my mum do all sorts for him. He didn't buy us presents, remember our birthdays, or contribute anything to the running of the house as far as I could see. All his money seemed to go on drugs and the idea of a father figure or role model was very alien to him, and therefore to me. His visits would leave all three of us on edge, and we were all relieved when he moved on again. I have no idea where he was the rest of the time. I imagine he was either crashing out at friends, or had other women he lived with too. I'm pretty sure he didn't actually have a place of his own, but if he did, he never told us about it or took us there.

Sometimes he would take me out, but it was very rare. We might visit other family or his friends, which I enjoyed as they often cooked great Caribbean food. But another time he took me along for a drive that I am pretty sure entailed buying drugs. Dad was never jailed for any involvement in drugs, but there is no doubt in my mind that he was a heavy user of cannabis. I remember clear as day the time he took me out in his gold Capri car – I know, who owns one of them?! – and pulled up alongside some people. He handed them money and in return they dropped a package through the window to him. He didn't explain anything to me and I knew better than to ask. It was just another thing that happened in life with Dad, and it was easier not to question any of it. To be honest I am not even sure I knew it was wrong at that age either.

I was at pre-school for a while, and was always getting injured. I played with the boys and was a real tomboy, but it meant I broke my ankle three times growing up, by jumping off things or playing where I shouldn't be. You would never catch me in dresses; I was always in tracksuits, and playing on my bike, or a scooter, or rollerblades. I loved adventure.

Then I began school at Carrington Junior School, and was relatively happy there as far as I remember. I went to church and Sunday school, sang hymns, and baked, and joined the Alpha group that was linked to the church as I believed in God for a while.

I joined lots of after-school clubs, and learnt to play the violin, and I had my fair share of friends whose houses I would go round for tea. We played cops and robbers and my favourite pastime on long car journeys was to pretend we were in a police chase and had to escape. Not sure what that says about the influences I was seeing around me, or the TV shows I was watching – step forward Jerry Springer and Maury Povich.

As far back as I can remember I had two really good friends called Rick and Cath. Cath had blonde hair and blue eyes, Rick had spiky brown hair and wore glasses. They were from West London and were teenagers when I was still at primary school, so were more like an older brother and sister. They didn't hang out with me when I was with any of my other friends, but would come over when I was alone. We would play together and chat about all sorts of things. They were always there when I was sad, and were really good at listening to my problems and always knew to visit me when I felt lonely.

There was only one problem – no one else ever saw them. Not my mum, my sister, or any of my friends, and I don't really know what to make of that. Maybe they were ghosts – all three of us have seen spirits, and there was definitely paranormal activity in my house growing up, but that is a whole other book! Or maybe Rick and Cath were a figment of my imagination. I guess that seems like the most obvious explanation, but they were so damn real.

Once I was a teenager I didn't see them any more. They didn't say bye, they just gradually stopped coming. Whatever they were though, they were there for me at times when I really needed a good friend.

Aside from them, I think my first real experiences of friendship were with the kids on the estate and from primary school. We would all just hang about together and play at each other's houses or in the street. I had friends, I did OK, but there were none that were especially great – or not.

My uncle Dennis (one of Dad's brothers) was a dancer and a teacher at the Jackie Palmer Stage School in High Wycombe. The school was set up in 1971 by Jackie, a West End dancer and choreographer, and her daughter Marylyn, and rapidly grew in size and reputation. A lot of very successful stars have passed through their doors over the years, including people such as Eddie Redmayne and James Corden.

When I was two, I enrolled there with the help of Uncle Dennis. In the beginning it was just half an hour a week, kind of a play class to encourage a kid's dramatic side to come out I guess, not that I needed it! Then it developed from there, and soon I was doing singing, dancing and acting lessons, and I loved it.

I don't think it mattered that I was mixed-race, in terms of my treatment by other people. I don't ever remember it being an issue at school, and actually High Wycombe is pretty multicultural. There are a lot of Asian and black people, and it was never really an issue.

The only arguments I ever saw to do with race were bizarrely within my own family. But the really important split there was not between black and white, but between men and women. I noticed, early on, that most of the women I knew had a really tough time of it, left to bring up the kids, struggling to make ends meet, without the support of their men. They were all constantly fighting to keep their heads above water financially and to do their best by their kids, but they got no thanks from their children's fathers, in fact they got quite the opposite.

The first time I remember hearing any domestic violence, I was six years old. I was really ill, and had a horrible fever, and kept throwing up. I was lying in bed watching a Noddy cartoon, when I heard men and women's voices, shouting and screaming in the next room, along with lots of banging. I was terrified, but crept out to see what was happening. One of my uncles had my auntie by the throat, up against the door, so I ran away again back to the safety of my room.

I won't go into detail about most of what I saw happening around me, out of respect for the innocent people involved. But believe me, I saw plenty. None of the women would ever go to hospital. I guess it was out of fear. They would just patch themselves up as best as they could. As a result none of the men were ever charged. It makes me sick that they got away with it. They will never say sorry or be punished, yet they damaged the lives of so many women and children.

As Dad never physically hurt me or my sister, I think Mum hoped that his behaviour wouldn't have much of an impact on us. But mentally and emotionally, Dad's abusive and disrespectful behaviour was having a huge impact on me. I could see, hear and feel it, and it cut right through me every time.

The men all dished out plenty of mental abuse too, which I found worse in a way. I'd hear them talk to the women like they were a piece of dirt on their shoe: 'Cook me my dinner, you fucking bitch.'

It was all about control and mind games, any attempt to make their pathetic selves feel more powerful, and on that front the kids did get dragged into it. Dad would be lying on the sofa with the remote next to him, and I'd be the other side of the room. 'Pass me the remote,' he'd demand, a test to see if I would obey whatever he asked.

I remember one cousin even had to wear a jumper to leave the house on a boiling hot summer's day, as she wasn't allowed to go out with any skin showing. To this day I don't know whether that was a controlling order for the hell of it, or if she was so covered in the bruises and damage that had been inflicted on her that her dad realised she had better hide it.

The only thing that helps explain their behaviour – it doesn't excuse it though, only helps give some background and context to understanding where it came from – was that they had grown up in an extremely violent household themselves. Their father apparently thought nothing of beating them regularly, so for Dad and his brothers, this behaviour was normal and acceptable. But let's face it, that's just bollocks, isn't it? How weak does that sound, to abuse a person and then claim you can't help but do it, as you are imitating your own parents? As far as I am concerned, once you grow up, you decide for yourself how to treat another person, and the way these men behaved was inexcusable.

I felt so sorry for Mum. I later found out she had been physically abused by her own dad as well, and was now having to put up with this from the father of her kids. The fear and sadness in her eyes whenever he turned up at the doorstep is what got to me more than anything. Although I suppose underneath it all, there must have still been attachment of some sort, even if it was unhealthy and toxic. Otherwise how did my sister come along five years after me?! No Mum, I don't believe it when you say the pair of you only had sex twice . . . Only two individuals can truly know what they feel for each other but all I know is that what I saw was not healthy or right. Growing up in that environment planted the message deep in my head that I would never stand for a man treating me that way.

Madness was a way of life for us. On one occasion, we were kidnapped by one of my relatives . . . I know how insane that sounds as I write it, and I have to laugh. HOW MESSED UP WERE MY FAMILY?! I am still not even sure of the reason for it, but it was something to do with him being angry that his car wasn't as good as someone else's, so when my family were around visiting in their house, he locked us all in, saying we would not be allowed out until his girlfriend got money off her family to get him a new one. I mean, come on, he was always banging on about being the man of the house, and yet he needed his girlfriend to buy him a new car? Absolute idiot.

So there we were, locked in for a whole week, with nothing to do. I was annoyed about it as I had to hand-wash my underwear as I had no other clothes up there. But at the same time it was a week off school, we had take-outs delivered to the house so we didn't starve and we just played games and hung out. It was such a weird situation to be trapped and in retrospect I can't believe the audacity of it. I don't actually remember how it ended, but I don't think the police got involved. I think at the time I just accepted it as another bizarre part of my family's behaviour and just cracked on with getting through the week.

Sometimes we would go on holiday to the south coast to visit Mum's niece Yvette and her children, who we got on really well with. After the dispute between Mum and her family over her choice of men, there seemed to be ongoing problems between them. We wouldn't be invited to weddings that all the rest of the family were attending and I can only assume it was because they disapproved of our mixed-race family, although I will never know for sure.

Yvette had made it clear she wasn't part of that way of thinking, and she and Mum were close. She had a house in Bournemouth, and it was like our little escape. My sister and I loved it. We had total freedom, and could go and play on the beach or have picnics, paddle in the sea, and hide out in the sand. It was great to be away from all the judgement back home, and it felt like we had real freedom. We would go for two weeks at a time in the summer holidays so it would be a real break and sometimes other aunties and cousins came with us. Dad and my uncles didn't like us going, though, and would stop us if they knew about it, so we had to be smuggled out of the house at 4 a.m., and driven away by Auntie Debbie to get us there before anyone realised we were gone. Charlotte and I were told very sternly that we weren't allowed to tell anyone that we were going away beforehand in case Dad found out and ruined it. Very hard for kids who are excited about a holiday!

Incidents like that pulled Mum, Charlotte and me together, and we would joke that we were the Three Musketeers, having to battle through life as a little trio who had each other's backs.

We weren't well off at all, and until we both went to school, we had to live off the benefits and tax credits mum was able to claim. After that, Mum would always take whatever jobs she could get between 8 a.m. and 3 p.m., which was mostly supermarket checkout work. She never let us know she struggled, and it wasn't like we ever went without the basics like clothes or food, it was just that there were no luxuries or designer gear. It was about getting by on a basic level, but that was all we knew, and what was going on with all the families around us on the estate, so Charlotte and I didn't even question it.

When I was thirteen we were moved to a new home, as under the council's rules my sister and I were old enough now to have our own rooms. The new place was about ten minutes away from the old place, and this time it was a house, a three-bed semi with a big garden and fields behind. That is where I lived the rest of my time in High Wycombe, and Mum still lives there today, with her boyfriend Kevin who she met when I was an adult, and who is ten times better for her than Dad was. #justsaying

Just before we moved I had been getting more and more wound up by Dad and the negative impact he was having on our lives. When my sister was about nine, this absolute state of a woman turned up at the door and got hold of Charlotte. This woman began telling her all about the sex she had with our dad in as much detail as she could. It turned out Dad owed her money, and this was her fucked-up idea of revenge. That was the kind of shit we had to live with, thanks to his involvement in our lives. It was pretty clear to all of us that he only ever seemed to bring trouble or bad feelings.

I don't think I allowed myself to think too much about my relationship with Dad – or lack of it – when I was that age, though. On the one hand, looking around at my cousins and the other kids on the estate, the way we lived was actually a relatively normal set-up. Hardly anyone lived in a neat family unit with a happily married mum and dad, living under the same roof. But other times I would visit friends from elsewhere, and see the set-up they had going on. Their fathers would be like alien crea- tures to me, eating dinner with the family, spending time with their wife and playing with the kids. The fact they were always there, and didn't create a sense of fear whenever they came into the room, was something I couldn't ignore. So yes, at times I did get angry with him, and disappointed that he was such a let- down. But mostly I tried not to let myself think about him.

Once we had moved, though, Mum said something that I thought was a great idea, and showed how keen we were to have him out of our lives. She said: 'This is our house, your dad won't ever have a key for it, as he is not welcome here. It is just for us.' I liked that plan. This was our home, a fresh start for us, the Three Musketeers, doing things our way, and not needing him to come along and get in the way and ruin things.

And true enough she must have had a word, because after the move he did leave us alone for a while, until one day I was up in my bedroom and could hear his voice from downstairs. He was kicking off at Mum and speaking to her like shit. All I could hear was his shouting, and as always it was like he just wanted to start an argument to show off his "manliness", or take out his anger on her, or whatever went on inside his stupid brain. It seemed like he always found a reason to belittle her and suddenly I knew I wasn't going to take this any more. Something inside me just snapped. I was not fucking having this.

I stormed downstairs and went straight up to him. 'Get the fuck out our house!' I screamed.

'What the hell?' He stared at me.

'I mean it. This is our house, not yours. Get out.' I jabbed my finger towards the door, and stared right back at him, daring him to do anything different.

I could almost hear Mum holding her breath behind me. It was the first time I had ever spoken back to him like that, and you know what his shocking response was? He turned round to Mum and said to her: 'You know why she is this way, all full of attitude? 'Cos she was raised by a white woman.'

Uh-uh, no way. 'Is that right?' I replied, still full of anger. 'Well, you laid down with a white woman and created me, so no complaining about it now. Now get out before I call the police.'

As I stormed over to the phone he chatted a bit more shit but, to our amazement, he walked out. Mum sat in shock, half laughing, half horrified, while I joined her, slightly euphoric from the adrenalin of it, and proud that I had finally taken a stand. Charlotte was not yet ready to take the same kind of stand though, and as she was only ten years old she was in shock about the whole thing. She was a bit too young to see or understand a lot of the stuff with our dad, and she would try and hide from it. I remember clearly she stayed up in her bedroom throughout this whole incident, crying in her bed.

When we talk about this period of our lives I am not even sure how much Charlotte remembers. Maybe Mum and I protected her from a lot of it, or she was just too young to take in what was happening. She only really knows a lot of it second-hand through us. But from that day it was like I became a bit of a protector. At fifteen I was the strong one in the family, and Dad never returned to the house after that. In fact I have hardly seen him since.

So was my home life unhappy? I don't really know. It was certainly all I knew. I think when you are a kid you just accept a lot of what happens around you. It is only when you get older that you look back and analyse stuff against what you know by then is 'the norm' and you are able to see what was missing or wrong. A lot of what you go through shapes you, but how you handle it can shape you too. It certainly all came back to haunt me later on anyhow, as you will see.

Seeking Help for Domestic Violence

Domestic violence can take many different forms and is an incredibly complex issue. I know from my experiences that not many families going through it try to get help. In my extended family, lack of trust that the police could actually do anything plus a fear that social services would get involved and take the kids definitely prevailed. But looking back I do wonder if things would have been different if any of my aunties had been willing to look outside the home for

help. I know now that there are plenty of places to go for
help even if it is to anonymously find out about your options
and rights, or just to have a friendly voice to listen to.

Women's Aid, for example, are an amazing charity who
work with survivors of domestic violence and their children,
to help them get out of their situation and start a new, safer
life. Their website is www.womensaid.org.uk.

Refuge is a national UK charity that provides a safe place for
women and children escaping domestic violence. They opened
the world's first safe house in 1971, which in itself horrifies me
because it was so recent. Before that, domestic violence was
very much seen as a private matter to be dealt with behind
closed doors. What is wrong with people! So thank goodness
for Refuge. Their website is www.refuge.org.uk.

Together these two charities run a twenty-four-hour
helpline for people in need of advice or help: 0808 2000 247.

A Lack of Role Models

Growing up, I never had a role model to look up to. There was no
one in my life who seemed like an older version of me, who had
succeeded, and who made me think, 'Yeah, you're sick, I want to
be like you.'

That makes me sad, as role models are so important to inspire
us to go on and do bigger and better things with our own lives,
and to help us reach our dreams and goals.

It doesn't matter who they are; they can be someone famous
or a woman who lives down the street from you. The important
thing is that you can see two things in them: something that you

associate with yourself, and something that you want to emulate, that will make you a better person.

It is natural to look for role models that remind you of yourself in some way. The people that prove not just that someone can do what they are doing, but that someone *like you* can do what they are doing. And that is where things fell short for me. The reality was in the late nineties/early noughties, there was no one for me to look up to who was like me – female, mixed-race, chubby, working-class background. Finding someone who ticked even a couple of those boxes was practically impossible.

In terms of race it felt like anyone black who appeared in newspaper stories was either a criminal, or involved in some other negative story. The only women of colour I can think of who were making a success of themselves were R&B singers, so you had people like Beyoncé, TLC and Mis-Teeq. But even then, I had a different skin tone to them, loose curls rather than Afro hair, and rolls, so they didn't really look like me.

Closer to home I wasn't really seeing any role models amongst people of colour either, although there was a general sense amongst other people my age that being mixed-race was kind of a cool way to be; it was celebrated as the best of both worlds.

Then there was the lack of curvy girls out there as role models, let alone properly plus size. You name me one news reporter, weather girl or television presenter who was more than a size ten at that time.

There was also no one in the public eye who spoke like me or my family. Even as a white woman my mum didn't associate herself with the well-spoken, middle-class people she saw on TV.

Anyone you spotted onscreen with a working-class accent was more than likely in one of the chairs on *Jeremy Kyle*!

It was becoming clear that anyone I saw who was like me wasn't exactly inspirational, and anyone inspirational wasn't like me. So it was in the back of my young brain that while I had all these dreams, there was no one in the public eye that I could aspire to emulate, who could send me the message that I could be who I wanted to be, and do what I wanted to do. So all the time I had these nagging doubts that maybe I wouldn't be able to achieve everything I wanted to, that perhaps becoming successful was not really a door open to someone like me, and maybe I was crazy even to try.

That absence of role models in my childhood and adolescence is one of the reasons I am keen to lead by example where I can, for people like me who are growing up today. Look at where I am today. If I can do it, so can you.

Chapter 2
PIZZA-CRUST NECK AND ARNIE ARMS

'I enjoyed being young but I would never relive
my teens. Those are hard years for everyone.'
Christina Aguilera

A gainst the backdrop of my family situation there was
another area of my life that dominated my thoughts. It
was beginning to shape who I was, and was the basic
reason for a lot of my rapidly developing insecurities – weight.

I was a pretty normal weight when I was born – 6 lbs 7 oz – and
continued to be so through my early years. It was only when I
started at school that I suddenly gained a few pounds and
became a bit chubby. I am not talking obese, though; look at my
baby pictures in the middle of this book, and you will see what I
mean!

In retrospect we didn't eat well as a family. I think it was
because we didn't have great access to lots of nutritious healthy
food. Partly that was thanks to the cost, and partly down to my
poor mum already juggling so much stuff she didn't have time to

cook loads of great fresh food from scratch (let's face it, I was also greedy, lol). People didn't seem to worry about processed and ready-made food being bad for you the way they do today. So we lived off meals like chicken nuggets with chips and beans. If we had been good, a trip to McDonald's was a treat. A lot of my friends would have been eating in a similar way, but for whatever reason I was the one who put on weight. It shouldn't have been a problem though; it was just a bit of puppy fat, combined with the fact I just loved my food! With exercise, a bit of lifestyle improvement and – crucially – a happy and confident mind, I'm sure it would have naturally dropped off over time. But no . . .

As my weight increase had been so sudden, Mum took me to the doctor, who began discussing me as though I wasn't there. He pointed out that I had a fat neck, which could indicate that I had a thyroid problem. So I had tests, and the results all came back to say no, there was no issue, my thyroid was fine, so it was left at that.

Except it wasn't fine. At six years old I had been told that I was overweight, so I now began looking around at other people. True enough, I was the biggest girl in my class. I thought some more about it and concluded that being fat was clearly a bad thing, otherwise why would I have needed to go to the doctor about it?

I started to take notice of issues around my weight at stage school, too. When we were measured up for outfits for shows, I realised mine was always the biggest size out of everyone's, and I would see other girls in their tiny little leotards, looking all neat and pretty. It didn't help that I have always been quite tall and had a large frame. I began to wonder why I couldn't be the same as them. I began studying my cousin Danielle, who was two years younger than me and had also started at Jackie Palmer's. She was very tiny and lovely, and everyone was always cooing over how cute she looked. I wanted that same reaction, but instead it felt like I was always put in the back row of the performers and left to my own devices.

I recently found a letter that I had written to my mum when I was nine years old. I think the main reason was to say thank you for my Christmas presents. But shockingly it shows that in amongst the childish thoughts filling my mind at the time, my weight was right up there. It said: 'Dear Mum, how are you? I'm OK. I hope by the summer I will have lost some weight. Thanks for the Christmas presents, I really liked them. I'm glad I am doing *Joseph* [the West End musical]. Love from Grace xxxx'

How bad is that? There I am discussing the usual things you expect a child to be talking about, and weight rears its head in the middle of it. A nine-year-old should not care about something like that, especially when I wasn't crazily overweight! It makes me really sad to read it.

At the same time I began studying my mum and her love/hate relationship with food. She has always been in great shape, but I would see that she would binge and then starve herself, yo-yo dieting throughout my childhood. One day she would literally be eating chocolate for dinner, the next she would spend the evening on her exercise bike, cycling like mad to get rid of the chocolate calories. In retrospect she had a pretty unhealthy relationship with food, but my aunties were the same. Food was their best friend and also their worst enemy. It gave them comfort and enjoyment but also a fear of gaining weight and looking fat. I am sure as I watched them, some of their attitudes must have rubbed off on me. We all pick up some of our relationship habits towards weight and diet from our mums at that age. I know that if I am ever a mum it is something I will be really careful about. I would want my daughter to learn positive messages about meals and weight, and to know that it is only important to be healthy; it is not size that determines the kind of person you are.

I'm not sure if it's factually true but to me it felt as if my weight steadily increased through my primary school years. I found it increasingly depressing and it was something I was ashamed about. When I went to secondary school I eventually asked for help from my mum and aunties in losing some weight and they agreed and weighed me. I was 9 stone. I was tall for my age, so actually looking back I am sure I was maybe a bit chubby but not the huge obese monster I felt I had become. It is hard for me to actually be sure, as by this stage I really believed I was fat and gross, so I only have the distorted image in my head. I have to look at any photos I still have from that time to get the real picture.

After that my family weighed me regularly but they would cover the screen so I never knew what the figure was, as my auntie said she didn't want me concentrating on what the scales said. Instead they took measurements of different parts of my body and said that I should focus on lowering those. I know at the time it was the fashion to look at inch loss rather than pounds and everything they were doing for me came from a place of love, but what I know now about body image, weight and mental health tells me this was the wrong way to go about it. It would have been more helpful to teach me about food and listening to my body rather than to become obsessively focused on appearance. But the world didn't – and doesn't – work like that. Everyone thinks if you are thin you are healthy and if you are fat, you need to do everything you can to sort it out.

Then two really cruel, hurtful things happened to me that sent my weight insecurities hurtling into another stratosphere. The first was inflicted by a man who should have known better, the second by a boy who was perhaps too young to understand the impact of what he was saying. Let's be nice and give him the benefit of the doubt!

My family had begun referring to me as fat and making jokes about my weight while I was still at primary school. Not my mum or sister, but Dad's wider family, but not dad, my uncles in particular. Their comments sank into my subconscious and began settling there as fact – as though 'fat' was an appropriate and accurate description of me.

One day when I was twelve and already feeling insecure, two of my uncles came round and sat on the sofa in the living room, smoking weed. I can picture every tiny little detail of that day. They had the door open as they wanted the smoke to go down the hallway and out the front door so the smell didn't linger in the flat. I was sitting, bored, on the floor, with nothing to do, so I was just aimlessly picking at the green carpet and listening to their chat.

Then one uncle looked at me and out of the blue said: 'You know you have a neck that looks like it is made of pizza crust, right? And your arms are so big they are like Arnold Schwarzenegger's arms. Arnie!' Then he started laughing and the two of them fell about, repeating the comments. I stared at them and felt my cheeks flush a bright, burning red. I tried to laugh along with them but I was horrified at the image they had conjured up and, feeling the tears starting to burn in the back of my eyes, I had to get up and walk out of the room. There was no way they were going to see that they had hurt me.

Whenever anything made me uncomfortable I always needed to get out of the situation. Then I would hide in the safe haven of my room or, if I was crying, the toilet, where I could wash my face in cold water and wait until it was no longer blotchy. My main feeling that day was shame. I tried to tell myself that I wasn't bothered by the comments, that they were just stoned and nasty and didn't mean them, but in reality I really took them to heart.

That night I studied myself in the mirror, pulling and pinching at my skin, trying to hold my head in different ways to slim my neck. I decided they were right, I was fat and horrible-looking. No wonder my life was crap; no one in their right mind would want to be near me!

As an adult I look back in horror at moments like that. Why did the people around me, those who were supposed to love and care about me the most, want to degrade me in that way? To make anyone, especially a teenage girl who is full of insecurities anyway, feel like shit, is just unacceptable. It was basically nasty bullying from men who should have known a lot better. Then again, given the way they treated my mum and aunties, I knew they didn't love or respect others, so it shouldn't have been a surprise. They hardly had a track record of being kind to people.

A few weeks later, I had a night out planned with my friends from stage school. As I always saw them as my closer and more real group of friends, I was really looking forward to it. I went down to the cinema with my cousin Danielle who had continued to keep her great, thin little figure as she had grown. She was really popular at the school with teachers and other pupils and the correlation between that and her weight wasn't lost on my weight-focused mind.

We met up in the foyer and I bought my popcorn and ticket for the show – *Spy Kids* I think it was. I still hadn't dated or kissed a boy yet, but there was one guy called Aaron Johnson in the group who I really fancied.

My first celebrity crushes were on Robbie Williams and Ryan Giggs (cringe, I know, I don't know what I was thinking either …). But they paled into insignificance compared with my huge real-life crush on Aaron. I had no chance of dating him, as he was one of the most popular boys in the school and everyone liked him, but still, I couldn't help it if I was yet another of his admiring fans!

While we were messing about before we went in, Aaron ran over to me and pulled up my top, exposing my stomach. 'Haha, look, you are fat!' he shouted, and started laughing. I froze and felt my cheeks flush as I pulled my top back down. I felt sick inside, but pasted a grin on my face and pretended it was fine. Laughing along was the only way I knew how to deal with it, but inside I was screaming, 'Why would you do that to me?'

The whole way through the film I felt sick with anxiety, and the popcorn I had bought sat untouched in my lap, tormenting me. *Why don't you eat me and get even bigger, you fat, ugly person. That is all Aaron thinks you are: fat and useless!*

I didn't take in any of the film, and as soon as we were out I pretended I had to be home. Getting back to my bedroom, I laid on my bed and cried into the night. I felt so utterly heartbroken and ashamed. I believed then more than ever that to be fat was one of the worst crimes you could commit. I felt as if it was all anyone saw when they looked at me and it was my weight that defined me. I thought about all the thin people I knew and how much easier their lives seemed. If only I could make myself more like them.

I wasn't getting an easy time of it at school either. When I had started secondary school – I went to Wye Valley School, although in my head I nicknamed it Why Bother School – I was tall, well developed, chubby and geeky. But in the beginning I had made friends with this great girl called Frankie, and we were really close. I accepted that I wasn't one of the cool kids, and we just got on with our own thing, doing our lessons and hanging out together.

I was pretty academic, at least in the classes I liked – English for the reading and story writing, drama for obvious reasons, and PSHE (Personal Social and Health Education) because I liked learning about sex and issues that affected people in real life (perhaps a sign of the direction I would go in!).

But Frankie was really badly bullied by the cool (read 'bitch') crowd, and at the end of Year Seven she moved to another school. I was sad to see her go and as I went into Year Eight I realised that suddenly I was being targeted instead by the bullies. It wasn't physical bullying, but relentless name-calling and mocking, anything to wear down their victim. I was called 'ugly' and

'Harry Potter girl', which in a way should have been a compliment, but it wasn't meant that way. My acting was just another reason to single me out.

Out of everything though, the most relentless focal point of the bullying was my weight. Any insult that would remind me and the rest of the world of the fact I was fat was reeled out at any opportunity. It was endless, exhausting and completely undermining.

There was also really pathetic general bullying, of the kind that gets teenage girls a bad reputation as total bitches. I can't believe I got sucked into it, but when you are at school and spend most of your life with these people, it is hard not to care about what they say and think. Example:

Beth during lesson one, asks casually: 'So, do you like Jasmine?'

Me, looking suspicious: 'Yeah, she's fine, why?'

Beth: 'No reason.'

Jasmine, storming over in lesson three: 'You bitch, you called me ugly!'

Me: 'What?'

Jasmine: 'Beth told me, how dare you?'

Me: 'What, I never said that, I ...'

It was like this ridiculous example of just how nasty teenage girls could be. Relentlessly lying, scheming, trying to put each other down, bullying . . . I felt sad and lonely and lost. It was clear I was fat, unpopular and simply not good enough.

It didn't help that we were getting to the age where boys mattered, and there was no chance any of them were going to give me the time of day.

Get Help for Bullying

It can seem as if being bullied is a rite of passage in some way, something that every child or teenager has to go through at some point. But that is not the case – we can actually all just be nice to each other, you know?!

If you or anyone you know is being badly bullied, there are places to turn. Obviously adults, teachers, etc. are the first ports of call, but in other situations try **Ditch the Label**, a Brighton-based anti-bullying charity who run campaigns as well as offering support, the majority of which is online and in chat rooms. Their key message is: 'No more disempowerment. No more prejudice. No more bullying.' Check them out at www.ditchthelabel.com or give them a call on 01273 201129.

Then something miraculous happened …

By the end of Year Eight at secondary school, I was desperate to date someone. People around me seemed to be dating left, right and centre, and were all paired off, but it just wasn't happening for me. Not that I was surprised, really. I was the chubby, glasses-wearing geeky kid, not exactly at the top of anyone's fantasy list.

Then a guy called Tom from stage school asked me out just as the school holidays began. I didn't fancy him, but I so badly wanted to say that I had a boyfriend when I went back to school in September that I said yes. I know that sounds awful, but I was a teenager, so come on, I am allowed. I just really wanted to be part of the group who had boyfriends.

So things were fine for a few weeks and Tom and I hung out together, mostly in a group, and held hands. But then on my birthday in August, on the ACTUAL DAY if you can believe the total cheek of it, he broke up with me. I was devastated. Not because I really liked him, but I hadn't even had a chance to tell people in school, and now I was facing the shame of being dumped. From an ego point of view I also couldn't work out why, as I was sure I had done nothing wrong.

As I sat wallowing in my misery, focusing on the fact that these bad things always seemed to happen to me, I got a phone call from Aaron – he of the top-pulling-up/fat-shaming incident. He wanted to check in and see I was OK and wish me happy birthday. Word clearly travelled fast as he also knew I was single, and said: 'I want you to know that I think Tom is a dick who shouldn't have broken up with you. I think you are beautiful.'

Wow, even as a thirteen-year-old, Aaron was smooth. It was incredible to hear those words. No guy had ever told me I was beautiful, least of all the most sought-after guy in stage school. I was shocked – as far as I was concerned he had made it very clear what he thought of my body earlier that year.

Then after all that, he asked me out. The most lusted-after boy in stage school, asked me, geeky Grace, out! I couldn't believe it, but obviously I said yes, and we began dating (Tom who?). That was the start of a whirlwind romance that was incredible, and gave me something really positive to look forward to every day. It didn't matter that I was having a shit time at school or being bullied; I was dating Aaron!

He was my first ever kiss, and it was the best fucking kiss ever! We were on a date at the cinema although I have no idea what the film was – I was too busy staring at him, thinking he was the most beautiful person in the world. He had his arm around me and at one point during the film he pulled me in to him and we ended up kissing. I realised half way through I was doing that classic first-time kiss move of having my eyes open, kind of half staring at him in shock, so I quickly closed them and was pleased I actually enjoyed it.

Yes, we were young, but I can honestly say I fell in love with him. We were inseparable. We would go to the cinema, out for dinner, and we would spend hours chatting on the phone. I had a mobile by then – a little basic orange Bosch one – which made life easier for privacy. We talked about anything and everything and he would sing down the line to me. As first boyfriends go, he did a good job of being pretty perfect.

Then suddenly, after four months of total bliss, it was over. It was just before Christmas, I was single again, and that was the end of my life. I went into shock as I hadn't seen it coming, and hadn't even begun to imagine life without him.

I remember the phone call practically word for word. At first Aaron started saying something about me having changed and the fact it wasn't really working. But then he admitted that he was actually about to be really busy with stage school work and had to go away abroad for filming, and because of that, we needed to break up. He said he had a lot on, and wasn't sure when he would be back to High Wycombe.

I couldn't speak. I was so overwhelmed by the sobs that were building up in my chest. Once I was off the phone I hid in my room and cried and cried.

I know we hadn't been together for long, but when you are thirteen years old, four months is an eternity. He had become my world and I was completely obsessed with him.

I think the saddest part that made it so difficult was that we hadn't fallen out of love, but he was telling the truth; his acting career really was on the up, and he had to go away to make his latest film. Before we had begun dating he had been in a film called *Tom and Thomas* about twins, and he played both of them. It was a lot of pressure for someone so young, but he had come out of it well, and it was clear he was definitely the stand-out person from our year at stage school who was going to make it big.

Sure enough, he has since gone on to be a really successful actor, starring in films like *Kick-Ass*, *Avengers* and *Nowhere Boy*. He also did *Angus, Thongs and Perfect Snogging*, and a bit of me thought our romance was like something out of that film. He is now married to director Sam Taylor-Wood and has changed his name to Aaron Taylor-Johnson. I haven't had any contact with him in the last few years, but I will always wish good things for him, and hope he is happy. You never forget your first love, and as first loves go, he was a pretty decent one!

At the time of our split, though, I was a broken person. Every insecurity about my body and my weight came crashing back in with a vengeance. I was permanently anxious and consumed by the idea that I wasn't good enough. Despite Aaron's very reasonable explanation I convinced myself he had left me as he didn't fancy me any more. I was ugly. I wasn't good enough. Worst of all, I was fat. As I laid in bed crying for the fifth night in a row, I decided I needed to do something about my weight, and fast. It had to be the reason I had been dumped, and this time I needed to tackle it. So I began making plans for how I could be skinny. I thought about all the people I knew who were thin, and the way they ate. It seemed they were all on these restrictive diets, so then and there I decided that was what I needed to do.

That very next day I began restricting my food. I would count the calories of every single item that was to pass my lips and obsess over any small way I could see to cut out food. At first it was a case of cutting out sauces, crisps, chocolates and sweets, and then I started skipping lunch. This meant that by the time I got to dance class in the evening I had an empty stomach and no energy, so would often shake and feel dizzy. It was clear I was harming myself, but I couldn't see it, I was so focused on the end result.

This was easy to do at school as no one would really notice what or if you were eating, but breakfast and dinner were harder, as we would eat as a family. Having said that, because Mum never made me feel that she loved me less for being bigger, I didn't worry about it as much at home. When it was just the three of us there, that was still my safe haven, so eating with her didn't give me the same pressurised feeling that I got when I was eating around other people. Then I would feel embarrassed and ashamed, as I felt like they would be analysing everything that went into my mouth and judging me for my size – and if they weren't, well, I certainly was.

So of course as a result of skipping lunch I started to lose weight. The changes were visible and people began commenting. One uncle even pointed it out – 'You've lost weight there, girl, you look good!' – but it wasn't dropping off as quickly as I had hoped. I wanted to be thinner, and quicker. And can you believe it, a couple of stretchmarks had begun to appear on my hips? What the hell?! There I was trying to get thinner, and they had appeared to taunt me, making me believe that I was getting fatter.

I began searching for ways online that could help me lose weight at greater speed, and wow, did I come across some crazy stuff. There are all sorts of websites out there full of extreme tips, comments that make you even more insecure, and dieting methods that basically help a girl very rapidly on her way to an eating disorder. And sure enough I soon read online about the way that some people throw up their food. This appealed to me as I was really missing eating, I enjoyed food, and although I was loving losing weight, it was making me sad to miss out on something that usually made me happy. I thought, wow, I can go back to eating whatever I want, then throw it up afterwards, and actually carry on losing weight quicker than I am now. That sounds perfect!

Of course I knew about bulimia through conversations at stage school, but in my mind this wasn't anything to do with that. Yes, I would be throwing up food, but I told myself I was fat, and only skinny, unwell-looking people have eating disorders, right? In my case I convinced myself it was just a method of dieting, and therefore a lifeline, even if I did make sure I was doing it in secret.

The first time I was sick was about midnight one night, when I was sitting in my room feeling heavy and fat. My dinner was sitting like a big lead weight in my stomach, and I was thinking of my regrets about eating it, and that I wanted rid of it. It seemed the right time to try out being sick, so I went to the bathroom, put my fingers down my throat and began retching, then finally I threw my dinner back up.

It was disgusting but not difficult, and after that I would do it regularly. In my head I was quite factual about it; I was simply getting rid of something that was not good for my body, so it was an action that needed to be done. I wouldn't do it after every meal, but it would often be late at night if I felt I had eaten badly that day. Or other times I would be sick in the toilets at stage school if I thought I looked bigger than usual in my outfit. I would end up with a sore throat, and my head would be spinning, but I wouldn't allow myself to acknowledge all the negative impacts it was having on my body.

Finding a way to throw up my food without people realising what was going on began to take over my life. I would plan out my day around ensuring that I had the free time and access to a toilet without disruption or questions. It meant I was becoming more socially isolated from others, and my mind was becoming consumed by it.

I don't actually know how much I weighed as I didn't use scales, and it wasn't the figure on that which mattered to me anyhow. The comments and attention from others was how I judged my weight loss, and was what gave the whole thing validation. After all, it was their criticism that had made me feel fat in the first place, so if they could make me feel thin, I would be happy, or so I thought.

At the end of Year Nine our classes had been switched around and, just my luck, I had ended up in a group with the worst of the bullies. But, incredibly, as my weight dropped off and I began to look like a new person, these girls were no longer mean to me, but wanted to be my friend! When they began complimenting my hair or my outfit, or wanting to hang out with me, I was initially suspicious, but then I saw that they meant it. While it made my life easier at the time it went a long way to confirm the message that I was already starting to believe – if you lose weight, things will be better. Your relationships will improve, people will like you, you will be prettier and more popular. They may as well have said to me the year before when they were bullying me: 'If you lose weight you can be friends with us.' I wonder what they would think now as adults if they knew how much psychological damage their cruelty inflicted on me back then.

I can't say I ever really considered those girls genuine friends, but I think I knew I needed to get on with them to make my secondary school years as painless as possible. I didn't like how they judged and bullied other people though, making their lives hell just because of their own insecurities. It is one of my few regrets in life that I never defended the people they targeted, but at the time I suppose I was just trying to get through and survive it as best as I could.

At the same time as my friendship began with them, I became more focused and confident on my looks in general and looking back – and giving the bullies the benefit of the doubt – perhaps it was the difference in my confidence rather than my weight that changed those around me. One of the first times Beth – who had originally been one of the bullies – was nice to me she came and sat next to me in a class and gave me her make-up bag. 'Let's ignore the teacher and try out this stuff,' she whispered.

And so we did. It was the first time I had ever properly experimented with make-up, and I remember the pink shimmery Bourjois eye shadow I chose. It was clearly horrific, but after that

I wore it all the time. I forgot about education and focused much more on my looks, and getting the body and face that I wanted.

It felt like even boys treated me differently once I had lost weight, and seemed to like me more, and accept me. I was invited out with them more often, and repeatedly I was getting the message: 'The slimmer you are, the better life is for everyone.' It was so ridiculous, and makes me angry to even write this. Society has some serious fucking issues that it needs to sort out!

Eventually it became apparent that I had taken my controlled eating too far, as a teacher at stage school called me in and asked me why I had no energy. I think she probably realised I was having issues with eating and wasn't sure how to address it. She didn't openly confront me, so when I shrugged, she told me to eat before I came to class and gave me some food ideas.

I tried to take on board what she was saying, as deep down I knew I was damaging my body, but the most important thing for me was not to be fat. I had become obsessed with changing the way I looked, and controlling my food seemed to be the best way to achieve that.

The problem was, like so many of the sticky plasters I have stuck on my problems over the years, it was just masking the real problems that I was refusing to face up to. The inner demons that I wasn't dealing with from my past. So after spending the day being one of the popular girls in school, I would head home to write dark poems about death, to throw up my food, and to wallow in feelings of insecurity.

The advice from my stage school teacher was the closest thing anyone came to addressing the issue, and in retrospect I am not sure why no one did confront me or try to understand why it was happening. Maybe they honestly weren't sure exactly what was going on, or more likely they didn't know how to address it. It is this fear of handling people with any kind of mental health issue that is one of the inspirations behind my blog. I want everyone to understand and help each other.

Making myself sick was something I continued to do on and off for a couple of years in my teens, but it phased out when a different area of mental health took over, as you will see in the next chapter. My issues with food and eating were to continue throughout my life though.

I only really accepted this period of making myself sick was actually bulimia when I was looking back on it from my twenties, and I feel sad that I put myself through it. I realise it is not often a conscious choice for people, but I would strongly urge anyone thinking of experimenting to avoid throwing up at all costs. It may seem like a quick fix, but you quickly lose control. The bulimia takes over and isolates you from other people, and is extremely unhealthy for both your mind and body. Ultimately, I can promise you it won't give you the answers you are looking for. Those can only come from self-acceptance, and tackling the real root of your issues – something I have only learnt myself in recent years.

Physical Side-Effects of Bulimia

According to the NHS, people who are bulimic not only need to deal with the mental issues surrounding the condition but also need to be aware that they are putting their bodies at risk of a lot of physical damage. The longer they continue without help, the more likely it is that they will cause themselves long-term harm. The most common problems are:

- All the acid passing through your mouth from being sick can lead to bad breath, dental problems and a sore throat.
- Periods can become irregular and even stop, leading to future problems in getting pregnant.
- Skin and hair problems are common, caused by a lack of nutrients.
- Saliva glands can become swollen from excessive vomiting, giving your face a rounder appearance.
- Chemical imbalances can lead to kidney problems, fitting, tiredness and weakness.
- People who use laxatives to help with weight loss can find they suffer with bowel problems and constant constipation.
- A crucial long-term effect of bulimia can be heart problems.

Chapter 3
I'M ONLY HURTING MYSELF

'Everyone wants to know how to be happy,
but I think learning about being sad is
much more useful.'
Daisy Buchanan

As I think you all know by now, I am an open person who can chat about pretty much anything, no matter how private or embarrassing I might think it is! But there is one chapter in this book I have been dreading writing, and it is this one. It is where I have to face up to a topic that I still find really difficult to talk about and that feels raw, as though I am exposing myself – self-harm. But deep breath, here goes.

There is something about the act of self-harm that I find incredibly sad. That a person can choose to cause damage and pain to themselves is awful. To know that someone has the desire to actually hurt themselves, and in such a way that can scar them for life both physically and mentally, is heart-breaking.

And yet, I have to hold my hands up and admit I have done that to myself repeatedly over the years.

I first self-harmed when I was fifteen years old. I was in a pretty dark place anyway, and had taken to going on social networking site Bebo and looking at depressing images and quotes from people going through a hard time. They weren't the kind of thing that people posted to cheer each other up; instead they were expressing their own pain and wanted people to understand, or to know that others were feeling the same.

I can't remember exactly what it was that triggered me on this particular afternoon, but I was sitting in my kitchen, alone and upset. I think maybe it was an MSN message or argument with a friend that had sent me into a dark place. I felt a gnawing sadness in the pit of my stomach, a sense of self-hatred and dislike of myself and my life, all twisting up inside me like a tightening knot. Normally I might have made myself sick to try to improve my mood. This was a different kind of pain, though, and something told me the release of getting my food back out wouldn't solve it this time.

So I decided I would try to hurt myself instead. I had read about different ways to do it on Bebo, but until that day hadn't really planned to try it myself. The most common was to cut yourself, and at that moment I realised that is what I wanted to do. I got a small sharp knife out of the cupboard and sat back down at the table. I rolled my sleeve up and studied my arm, then with a deep breath, I sliced across my skin. It was a sharp knife and didn't take much pressure, and I watched, fascinated, like an outsider looking at the arm of another person. I kept cutting at the same bit, creating a row of lines, and as the blood oozed to the surface, I felt a sense of release. Although it obviously hurt, it felt as though that surface pain was helping to draw out the deeper pain from inside me.

After that day, cutting myself became part of my coping mechanism. If I felt sad, depressed, frustrated, angry, any sort of negative emotion really, I would find myself a quiet corner and something sharp – a knife, compass, scissors, blade of any sort, it didn't matter, as long as it could cut. When I was at a particularly low point, I was cutting myself every day, or if things were going better, it could drop to once a month. I would always choose a place on my arms or my legs, where I could hide the scars from people, for example my upper thighs, or parts of my arms that could be covered with tops. I also made a point of never cutting deep enough that I would have to go to hospital, or where it could leave serious scars, as I didn't want people to know what I was doing. A bit like with throwing up my food, I made sure to hide it.

I also took to scratching myself with my nails. It would cause the same stinging pain, draw blood, and create the same sense of release, but there was very little chance of long-term scarring. I would also pick at old cuts, and open up wounds, watching the blood come back to the surface, while the cut stung.

Writing this I am cringing as I realise how awful it sounds, and I understand how hard it is for people to understand if they haven't gone through it, or spent time educating themselves on it. But research has shown that the sense of release that feels so good is a genuine thing. The closest thing I can think of to describe it is when a child has a tantrum and screams and cries. Have you noticed that afterwards they often become really relaxed and mellow, and more than likely fall asleep? Self-harm has a similar impact on the person.

There is definitely a preconception that people who self-harm hate life and are suicidal, but in the majority of cases this is not true. You maybe hate an aspect of your life, or something you are going through, or don't even know why you need to cut to cope, but often people are doing it because they *want* to live, and to do so they need to feel something, to get that release, and then heal.

I think the main attraction of it for me was that I had no one to blame for a lot of what was happening in my life. My dad was never around, so I couldn't blame him, but I loved my mum, and it wasn't her fault. So instead I internalised it, and while I didn't realise it at the time, it was sitting in me, eating away at me, creating a growing pressure.

When I cut myself it released this and matched up the pain I was feeling on the inside of my body with the outside. If someone hurt me, I would hurt myself. It became as much a reaction and part of my life as how if I felt thirsty, I would drink some water.

When I began to get panic attacks later in my teens, the self-harm instantly brought me back from that crisis stage. The physical pain calmed the emotional pain.

Self-harm as a term actually refers to a much wider spectrum of behaviour than just cutting yourself. Anything that is effectively injurious to yourself, which is caused by self-destructive thoughts, can be described as self-harm. So some people will pull out their hair, hit themselves, or bash their heads against the wall. This last is more common among guys, as it can easily be hidden behind the excuse that they got into a fight, or fell over during a game of sport. Then there is the fact that under that definition, when you numb the pain with alcohol or drugs, or binge eat, or have unprotected sex because you are in a period of deep self-loathing, this is also classified as self-harm.

Some people put tattoos and piercings under this category too, although I disagree there. For me those are fun, and about looking good, although I can perhaps see that for the odd person who has taken them to the extreme, it is about the pain that comes with it, and changing their bodies. I think the source of the behaviour is what is important. If it comes from a negative place, if you need to hurt yourself as a release, then this is a problem, and you are self-harming and need help. We all need a release, but it should be done in a safe way.

Self-harm, the Statistics

- Because self-harmers are generally so secretive, it is hard to know how many people are actually going through this. According to charity selfharmUK, the estimate is that 13 per cent of people try to hurt themselves at some point between eleven and sixteen years old, but this figure could be much higher.

- In 2014, the number of ten- to fourteen-year-olds who had gone to A&E for self-harm-related reasons was 70 per cent higher than the two years before, implying it is on the increase.

- Girls are believed to self-harm more than boys, but this may be because a boy's chosen method may be less obvious to a hospital as self-harm, or not recognised as that by those around him, e.g. punching a wall.

The problem for me was, like so many self-destructive behaviour patterns, self-harming was one big downward spiral. It would work at the time, but afterwards I would feel a horrible gnawing guilt, and the self-loathing would come back stronger than ever. It became an extension of who I was. But in much the same way that people numb pain with alcohol and drugs, I soon realised this release was only temporary. By that point I was too deeply reliant on it, though; I was addicted to the self-destruction.

It continued on and off for several years as part of my mechanism for coping with life, and only really faded out altogether when I reached a happier stage in my early twenties. By then I had learnt other ways of coping, and had new focuses, goals and responsibilities that kept my mind otherwise occupied.

Sadly, I think that once you have gone down the self-harm route, it will always stay with you. It will always be a part of you, so it is about managing it. I think that is why I struggle to talk about it more than anything else in my life. My skin actually heals really well, so the upside of that is that today I don't really have many scars that people can see. On my left arm you can see a few if I am wearing fake tan as the tan doesn't attach as well to scar tissue (yes, before you say it, I know I am mixed-race, but I hate looking beige so I wear fake tan, all right?!). But I have musical notes tattooed on to cover the more obvious scars near my wrist. I have seen people with really deep scars years later, and in some ways it is a sad reminder, but we all unfortunately carry the mental scars.

Years after it had happened to me, I had a care job and as part of that I was put through a course on dealing with self-harm. I was taught techniques to help self-harmers find alternative ways to cope without actually harming themselves. I eventually used some of them myself, and found them very useful. A few of them were:

- Flicking a hairband or elastic band on your arm can give you the same slight stinging sensation that cutting will, and is a safe way to inflict minimal pain.
- Get a red marker pen and draw lines across your arm in the place you like to self-harm. It gives the illusion of blood and your mind will read it like that and react accordingly.
- Open a window or go outside. Fresh air does wonders and can make you feel like you are less trapped.
- Write down how you feel (in red pen if you like) so that your brain can free up some space to let some positive, less destructive thoughts in.
- Practise mindful breathing. Breathing in and out in counts of eight or ten will calm you down and provide some relief.

For anyone who hasn't self-harmed but may be thinking of it, PLEASE DON'T. If I could go back in time I would make myself realise that those online suggestions of self-harm were very dangerous and I would never have let myself pick up that knife the first time in the kitchen. It is like a drug addiction where you get pulled into a parallel world and the need to cut overtakes everything else. In the meantime, it impacts on your life, your thoughts and, of course, your body.

Even now at particularly negative points in my life I have to contend with the little voice in the back of my mind that says:

'Pick up that knife and push it into your skin. Go on, you know how much better it will make you feel.'

And I do know, but I also know that the relief is temporary, and the effect permanent. More importantly though I don't hate myself any more in a way that I would want to inflict that kind of damage. You wouldn't dream of hurting a friend with a knife, so the idea of doing it to yourself should be equally as horrifying.

I love and respect myself enough that I never want to put my body through anything like that again, and I hope that anyone going through self-harm right now, or thinking about it, instead learns to love themselves too and move away from it.

Seeking Help for Self-Harm

Self-harm is a very solitary thing, and a lot of the time very few people, if any, will know what you are going through. But as with all mental health problems, it is good to talk to someone about it. Friends and family are always the first place to turn, but if you would prefer a stranger, or you need further help regardless, have a look at these places:

- **SelfharmUK** is a good place to start if you are looking for help for yourself or another person, general information and understanding, or you are looking for training for a deeper understanding of the issue: www.selfharm.co.uk.

- **Childline** is a good source of information and has counsellors available to chat twenty-four hours a day. It is run through the NSPCC, and you can call them on 0800 1111, or chat one-on-one with someone online: www.childline.org.uk.

Breaking the Taboo

Self-harm is still one of the least discussed and most taboo mental health issues, but luckily some brave famous people have begun to speak out about their experiences, which I can only see as a good thing.

- **Demi Lovato** revealed her battles with self-harm and eating disorders in an MTV documentary, saying she had made the decision to speak out as she still felt extremely vulnerable, but hoped that another sufferer would take hope from hearing her story.

- **Kelly Holmes** has talked candidly about slashing herself with scissors when she was training as a runner for the Olympics and under immense pressure. She said: 'I don't think it gave me any release. It was just hating myself and my body at that time for letting me down.'

- **Megan Fox** has previously admitted to cutting herself, but has avoided elaborating for fear of becoming a role model.

- **Russell Brand** admitted in his autobiography that he has regularly self-harmed since childhood, revealing that in his lowest moments he slashed his arms and smashed a glass to cut his chest with.

- **Johnny Depp** revealed he cut himself as a teenager to deal with his parents' divorce.

- **Angelina Jolie** has talked about cutting herself from the age of fourteen. 'I went through a period that when I felt trapped I would cut myself. I have a lot of scars.'

- **Cara Delevingne** admitted she would hit her head against a tree 'to try and knock myself out' as a teenager.

  Other celebrities reported to have self-harmed include Lindsay Lohan, Drew Barrymore, Colin Farrell, Owen Wilson and even Princess Diana.

Chapter 4
THE INTROVERTED EXTROVERT

'The greatest light comes from the darkest places.'

There is one very weird thing about me that you should know. Well, lots of weird things actually, but for the purposes of this chapter, I'll just give you one! You may already be wondering about it – the two totally different sides to me. There's the Grace who needs to hide away in her bedroom, and who worries all the time about what people think, and if she is good enough. Then there's the Grace who loves stage school, confidently models her latest outfits, and chats happily to thousands of strangers.

I know you must be sitting there reading about how I hate the way I look, or how I have cried alone in my bedroom racked with painful insecurities, and scratched your head, going, 'But you talk about your love of performing, and you have chosen a career where you have completely opened yourself up to be judged. What's going on?'

I get that it is hard to connect the two so I will try to explain it.

I've learnt that you can be both an introvert and an extrovert and, well, I think that is me. The reality is I am a bit of both, and that is no bad thing. Best of both worlds!

I do sometimes wonder if the mixture partly comes from when I was young, when I still didn't know who I was or what I wanted to be, when I was still unformed. Up until you are anything between three and five years old, adults can almost determine what you are like and give you a role, and then you try to fulfil that, then over time it becomes part of you. I'm not sure if that is right, but I do think as a kid because of drama and the fact I was confident on some levels, adults decided I was an extrovert. Maybe I learnt how to give off an extrovert impression, and partially became one over time. I certainly learnt to be loud, laugh, mess around and entertain.

An Introvert: *Someone who enjoys solitary activities, is reflective and reserved and prefers interaction with a small number of individuals. Not to be confused with shyness.*
An Extrovert: *A person who thrives off human company, takes pleasure in social gatherings, works well in a group, and becomes bored when alone.*

There is no doubt that stage school is responsible for much of my larger-than-life, outgoing personality. I took to performing like a duck to water, whether it was on stage, behind a camera, or just in front of the teacher and class. I have always had immense belief in myself as an actress, a singer and a dancer. I can't particularly explain why, but for whatever reason I do trust in my

talents and abilities – it is more confidence about my appearance that has forever been the negative voice in my head. I think
perhaps that through all the craziness of my home life growing
up, performing was the one constant that kept me totally happy
and grounded. It took me away from everything in my family life
and the madness in our flat, and off to a place where I could be
whoever I wanted to be. Because that is definitely key to it – *whoever you want to be*. I could put on whatever front I wanted, and
then it wasn't actually Grace being judged there, but the person
I was pretending to be.

At home we had a balcony in our flat that overlooked the
estate, and I used to treat it as my stage. I would be out on it performing songs such as 'Genie in a Bottle', pretending I was
Christina Aguilera, and people passing or living opposite
would watch me. I wanted to be a pop star and I was a total
show-off!

Deep down I think I was desperately ambitious from an early
age and wanted so badly to make a success of myself. When I
was eleven my singing teacher at stage school, a guy called Tom
(we always called them by their first names), told me something
I will always remember. 'Grace, I think you are going to be a star
when you are older. I'm not sure what you are going to be, or
how you are going to get there, but everyone is going to know
who you are, I'm sure of it!'

It was such a lovely thing to be told and gave me a great confidence boost to get out there and actually give things a go.

There was an agency attached to my stage school, and I would
get lots of jobs through them. Whether I was in front of the

camera to model, dance, sing or act, it was like escapism, and gave me a focus and a release.

I also got a role in the ensemble for the musical *Joseph and the Amazing Technicolor Dreamcoat* when I was nine. Initially it was on in the West End, and we would travel in three nights a week to take part in performances. Later it moved to High Wycombe and then Oxford, and I carried on doing it for seven years on and off. During the time I was there I remember a few famous faces being cast as Joseph, including Stephen Gately, and H from Steps. It was great fun as other people from my stage school were also in it, so it didn't seem a chore, with all of us going together. And really it was an escape from the trauma I was going through at home, whether that was the violence, Dad's absence, or the bullying. That stuff happened in High Wycombe, this stuff was in a different place, and it was a way out, a different life.

I was paid for my performances and although it was never much, the money was put into a bank account for me to access when I was sixteen, which gave me a sense of independence.

Over the years I was also in TV shows like *Family Affairs*, *The Bill*, a BBC series called *Big Kids*, and some bits for Tiger Aspect Productions. But my favourite filming experience ever began when I was ten years old and I was asked if I would like to be put forward for a new Warner Bros film that needed plenty of extras. I agreed, went for auditions, my measurements were taken, and then I was offered a part on the film – *Harry Potter and the Philosopher's Stone*, the first in the Harry Potter series.

I wasn't a main character and did not appear on screen that

often. My role was as one of the other kids at school, but keep your eyes peeled and you can spot me next to Hermione and Ron.

It was filmed at the Leavesden Studios near Watford in Hertfordshire, and was the best experience of my whole life. It was long hours on set, so we had tutoring there as we were missing a lot of school. There was so much freedom to it. There were fridges round the studios where you could help yourself to food and drink (probably to blame for my love of Custard Creams), and we would all just hang out, no drama. It was a world away from the problems I was having at home and that were about to begin at school.

After that, I was called back again for three more of the Harry Potter films – *Harry Potter and the Chamber of Secrets*, *Harry Potter and the Goblet of Fire*, and *Harry Potter and the Order of the Phoenix*, finishing the last one when I was fifteen. The whole cast were brilliant and I would love to do something like that again.

While I was on set I was definitely sassy, full of confidence and in extrovert mode. Occasionally, though, the insecurities from my everyday life did rear their head and in all sorts of ways, such as the time I flashed my knickers at Daniel Radcliffe. Yup, I did just say that. Harry Potter got a proper eyeful of my floral pants. Lucky lad!

On this particular day we were filming for a scene for the *Goblet of Fire* when we were getting into boats to travel into Hogwarts with our teachers. I was fourteen at the time, and we were filming in Virginia Water. I was wearing beige trousers and floral knickers, and of course our boat was the one that capsized. As we were pulled out of the water, I was mortified to realise that my trousers were now pretty much see-through. I couldn't have chosen a worse day for that underwear – but how was I to know everyone would soon get an eyeful? I felt exposed. I was no longer in character and I was aware that everyone was staring at me, Grace, standing there, looking ridiculous. At moments like these, other people could laugh and shake it off, but not me. My mental health and body image issues would come slamming in full force, and taint my attempts to downplay it in my head.

'Are you OK?' asked a concerned Daniel Radcliffe. 'No!' I said, embarrassed, upset, and unsure how to cope. He let me into his trailer to get dried off and sorted, and soon I began relaxing, falling back into the role of Grace the actress. We ended up hanging out there for ages, just chilling out together. He is a great guy and the right person to be around in that situation. Luckily today I now laugh about it; I mean who else can say they flashed Daniel Radcliffe and got invited into his trailer for their efforts?!

Despite all the acting, it was dancing that was really my passion. By the time I was at secondary school I was doing twenty-four hours of dance classes a week. I would do tap, ballet, jazz, hip-hop, contemporary salsa, even gymnastics. Out of them all, contemporary was my favourite as you can do the weirdest moves, but still look amazing. The only one I hated was ballet. That is all about poise, and you have to be dainty and light-footed for it, and that just ain't me.

To this day nothing gives me the feeling that dancing does. It really is just the best thing in the world. It is a way of expressing yourself, taking yourself to a different place. You can be any colour, any size, and still be great at it. I wish I had known back then that it is nothing to do with how you look, it is all about how you perform. I knew I could dance but I hated my body in a leotard, and too often focused on that.

Insecurities about my appearance would always bring out the introvert in me. So one minute I could be messing around being stupid, the loudest in the room, and the next we would be changing into our leotards for dance class, and I just wanted to curl up inside myself. Any wish to be in the middle of a crowd disappeared. But my desire to do well was so strong that at times like that the extrovert would trump over the introvert and I would push on. I think we should all try to beat our demons. If you are strong enough to stand up to your fears then make sure you do.

Same goes for modelling and photoshoots. Give me a job to do and I go into serious extrovert mode, which is useful, as that is what they want when they book someone for these kinds of jobs. They want a girl who is bubbly, passionate, full of life, confident and ambitious.

But with all these types of activities, ever since I was a kid, I am completely emotionally drained by the end. I always need to go home and lock myself away in my bedroom to recover. I need time just to myself, to watch TV, unwind, and not have to speak to anyone. I want to just withdraw inside my own mind and be left alone.

Interestingly, I think a lot of the kids at stage school were perhaps the same, and it was yet another reason we bonded so well and understood each other. I wasn't close to my school friends – while I wanted to spend my evenings and weekends at drama school, they were out smoking and drinking – but I always felt like I had something in common with the people at stage school.

There was a very set group of us – me, Roz and Lauren were the girls, then the boys were Tom, Luke, Jack, Marvyn and Beno. Our mums were all friends so they were happy for us to spend lots of time together outside of stage school as well. We would have sleepovers, house parties, order Chinese and drink WKD . . . When we got to the age when everyone was starting to fancy each other, we would play spin the bottle and end up kissing each other and fancying a different one of the boys each week! But we never argued and were able to be ourselves.

Aaron rejoined our group when he came back from filming – and he wasn't wrong about not knowing how long he would be gone for as it was pretty much two years! I remember his return, which happened without warning. He just walked into stage school one day when I was in the middle of a dance routine. I stopped dead, feeling exposed in my skimpy dance outfit, and my jaw just dropped as I stared. I knew everyone was looking from him to me, as our whole relationship had been played out through stage school and it was a nosy gossipy place anyway. I was like, 'Don't any of you look at me or say a word to me!'

I guess I still kind of fancied him, and once after a few drinks we started talking about our time dating and how we had split. Aaron started crying and apologising, then things got a bit heated, but we never rekindled anything and the reality was we were better as friends and he completed our group nicely.

I liked that it made no difference that we all came from completely different backgrounds. Some of them were from really rich families, others came from poorer backgrounds like mine, but actually none of us kids were materialistic, so it didn't matter. I was able to be myself with them. We were all also really focused on our dancing and acting, and getting jobs, whether on TV or in the West End.

Despite the competitive nature of what we were going into, we were all supportive of each other, and there wasn't much judgement. If one of us got a role or was successful, the others would all be genuinely pleased for them. These were the people who I actually enjoyed hanging out with, and who shaped my idea of what friendships should be.

Back in regular school, I was also learning confidence and self-belief from a lady who was an absolute legend, and my first real role model. Ahh, yep, looking at you, Mary McCrystal! She was my Religious Studies teacher and I loved her because she was different to all the other teachers. Her lessons were not about her standing at the front of the class and lecturing us about the different religions. Nor would she spend the whole class writing on the board, instructing us to sit there copying it into our note-books, not taking a thing in, but quietly dying of boredom while we developed a hatred of the lesson . . . as 'may' have happened in some of the other classes! No, she was all about debates and discussions, and encouraging people to have opinions, ask questions, and not be afraid to express their thoughts. And of course much of it was on religion, but it also crossed over into social issues and topics that might have been considered taboo or too risqué elsewhere. We talked about things such as the role of Islam – I got so interested in the religion at one point that I even thought about converting – and about war as the Iraq war had just begun and was the basis of a lot of debate.

Mary was smart, witty, and drew the extroverted side of me out, in a positive way. I thrived in her class and learnt to challenge opinions and feel confident in my own beliefs, as well as working out exactly what it was that I was interested in. I was inspired by her and feel that she really added to the person I have become today. I am friends with her on Facebook ten years on from leaving school, which shows how much of an influence she was on me – how many other people can say they are still friends with one of their high school teachers today?

The two different sides to my character - extrovert and introvert - continued as I got older. I think when someone dresses and talks the way I do, people assume I am the life and soul of the party, that I like drinking and socialising. They assume that because I am pushing ahead with my career and talk passionately on certain subjects, I am confident and outgoing and that because I am quite a people's person I must be an extrovert.

To a point they are right but I have my limit, when I just need to escape. When the idea of talking to one more person or being at another busy event terrifies me. When being asked to stay and socialise away from the safety of my home for another couple of hours literally brings me out in a sweat.

I am happy in silence and don't like too much small talk, as I feel like a lot of people actually drain me. I only have a set amount of energy that I can give to other people, and I feel like I am wasting it if I give it to random people. I try and reserve it for myself, or those who really matter.

More often than not I actually need to be at home recharging. Sitting with my own thoughts and relaxing with just myself or one or two friends for company. Having my own space is an actual physical need, and if I don't get it I can get very anxious. I love just putting on an inspiring film that I have watched a hundred times before, and just letting the words I know off by heart flow around me, while the empowering message sinks in, and my thoughts can float off elsewhere.

My Favourite Empowering Films

My top empowering watches of the moment:

- *The Other Woman*
- *The First Wives Club*
- *The Help*
- *Enough*

Despite my quiet periods, I think I attract people who like extroverts, with my big laugh, openness in conversation and ability to mess around and have fun. But then they think I must be a larger-than-life character all the time and I feel like I disappoint them when they see that I'm not. When they suggest meeting up, I would rather they came round to mine for an evening of Netflix and one-to-one chatting than hit the latest bars and parties. They misunderstand me and assume I am an extrovert through and through, when I am an extrovert on the surface and an introvert at heart. I worry it is why I make friends easily but struggle to keep them.

Maybe it is the mixture of my personality that makes YouTube work so well for me. I am able to socialise with a huge range of people, chatting, joking and having fun. But I am doing it from the safety of my own bedroom, and if it all becomes too much, all I have to do is flick a switch and I can retreat back to the safety of my own company. It is like being at a party with the perfect exit strategy. Because I do have a strategy, every time I go to an actual event or party! I know how I am going to leave if it gets too much. It isn't always too clever a strategy though – most of the time it is just a case of it's midnight, I'm done! Everyone's too drunk to notice, so I'll just get up and walk out and not say 'bye' in case it becomes a big deal. It's how I manage it. It is also why I rarely stay at people's houses after nights out, as I just need to get home and chill in my flat. That is probably why I have never lived with friends either. The idea of coming home after a day of meetings and events then having to talk to flatmates? Noooooo. That would be too much. I am literally incapable of speaking by then, and company would just stress me out.

If I am sad my introvert side becomes more dominant, again I guess to look after me.

There is an element of self-protection to this side of me, I think. Out working, facing criticism and comment, or giving a talk to a group, of course I need to be an extrovert to hold it together and to give people what they are after. Back home, the introvert allows me to recover, to take care of myself. Clothes off, make-up away, I guess I am essentially naked and vulnerable. A normal person who wants to be alone.

Signs You Are an Introverted Extrovert

There are plenty of signs that point to a person being an introverted extrovert, and I think the important thing is to embrace it, if this is you. Don't pretend to be something you aren't, but accept what makes you happy and works for you. I have found all the below descriptions apply to me, so these days I don't fight it, but I do what I feel is right for me in each situation.

- You love being the life and soul of the party, but need your own time before and after to psyche yourself up, and then recover. There is no way you wouldn't be at the centre of the action while there, but it is draining too, being permanently in extrovert mode, so you need to make sure your batteries are totally charged up before, and can be recharged after.

- You always have an escape plan in place. Although you can generally cope with any social situation, you need that one emergency action plan plotted out, in case it becomes too much and you need to get out of there, and fast.

- Although you like being social, and want everyone to think of you as that person, secretly there are plenty of nights when you would rather be curled up at home on the sofa with a throw, take-out, and just you and your favourite film for company.

- You find it easy to make casual friends, but harder to find the deeper, more meaningful friends who you can trust, and they are the ones that really matter to you. But while they are few and far between, when you get one, you hold on to it and appreciate it.

Chapter 5
I OWN MY BODY, NOT YOU

'This is not a sad story, this is to show you how I
returned from the darkest of days, because
they cannot win.'

I would say I have worked through and dealt with all the
issues and traumas that I talk about in this book, or I was
dealing with them through therapy as I sat down to write.
That is to say ... everything except what you are about to read in
this chapter.

This is a period of my life that I assumed was over. I had buried
the memories so deep I couldn't access them, so I figured they
must be a thing of the past. But starting to even allow myself a
glimpse of what happened so as to be honest with you lovely
people, I realise I had actually just disassociated myself from this
particular event, and hadn't processed it at all.

Cue a rapid therapy stint!

Although I have hardly told anyone since this thing happened
in 2006, I want to put it all down here as it is crucial to the person

I am today. I have also sadly become more and more aware of the number of people who have gone through similar experiences and, as with so many of these topics, the more we can all talk about them openly, the less taboo they become, and the more empowered we all are.

When I finished school at sixteen, I went on to dance college. Right from the start I didn't like it much – there was a lot of paperwork and written tasks, when really I wanted to get on with the actual dancing. So I kept myself quite distant from the people in my class and instead I hung out with other friends I had met outside of college, who looking back were basically the kind you would describe as 'the wrong crowd'. They were all a year or two older than me, and smoked weed and snorted cocaine (I didn't join in, BTW!).

One day in autumn 2006, one month after I had begun college, one of the girls asked me if I wanted to hang out with a couple of guys she had met online. I said yes.

She drove us to a college campus some miles away, where we met these two guys at the student halls and just chilled out in their room. The other three all smoked weed and got drunk. Then my friend and one of the guys ended up having sex while me and the other guy just carried on chatting.

The following weekend my friend suggested we do the same thing and I agreed. As I was waiting to be collected by her she said she was running late so would ask the lads to pick me up and she'd meet me there if she could.

I don't remember their names but one of the guys picked me up from the end of the road I lived on. I didn't give him my exact address because something in my gut told me not to. Again we drove to his university halls where his friend met us. There was only one chair in the room so I sat on the bed, drinking a Diet Coke that they gave me.

Then things began to get a bit hazy. I remember the guy who had driven me coming over to kiss me, and I felt uncomfortable, but just went with it. He started to grab my legs and said to his friend: 'Have you ever seen thighs like it?' in an admiring voice. A bit of me liked the compliment because as I think you know by now they are one of my most hated body parts, but another bit of me didn't like the way I was being talked about like a piece of meat. I was out of my depth and I knew it.

I felt very vulnerable, a bit sick, and was starting to get scared. Something in my gut was telling me the situation was getting out of control, and I needed to leave. But while I was trying to work out the best way to get out of there, the room began to get a bit hazy, and I started feeling dizzy. As I looked round to try and get a grip on things, *BAM*, a darkness came in.

I don't remember anything more until I came round to find the first guy on top of me on the bed, having sex with me. I tried to speak, to tell him to get off me, but I couldn't form the words. I wanted to push him off, but my arms wouldn't work. He was strong, hairy and sweaty, everything I dislike in a man, and he was saying something to his friend in a foreign language that I didn't understand.

I managed to turn my head to the side and I remember it was foggy outside and there was mist on the windows. I had no idea what time it was, but it was dark, and orange street lamps were shining through the window, so I tried to focus on them and block out everything else.

I was in and out of consciousness so I don't know how long it lasted, but the next thing I remember is being on the floor, with the second guy on top of me. I was beginning to come out of the haze and managed to get the word 'no' out. He was even stronger than his friend though, and when I tried to squirm from under him, he punched me.

I was coming back to myself more and more by the minute, and it seemed like the sex was over pretty quickly. As I tried to sit up one of them turned to me and said: 'You fucking slut bitch, you made my friend cum more than me.'

I couldn't speak, but just looked down, overcome with shame and fear. His comment made me want to curl up and die.

The experience seemed to be over but I wasn't sure, and was afraid they would want more from me. So with my legs now beginning to function again, I grabbed my jeans and hoodie and ran out. They didn't try to stop me, and I stumbled out onto the campus grounds, naked, desperately trying to pull my clothes on.

I started to walk, not knowing what direction to head in or what I was looking for, I was dazed, confused, and in shock. There was no one in sight, and I tried to pull my thoughts together. I know it sounds weird, but calling out for help or ringing the police didn't cross my mind. I was entirely focused on figuring out a way to get home, back to the sanctuary of my bedroom. All I wanted was to be in a place where I felt safe. That alone was my all-consuming thought.

I'm sure it didn't help that I was still groggy and couldn't focus. I can only assume looking back that they had put some kind of drug in my Diet Coke.

After walking around for what felt like hours but may only have been minutes, a car pulled up next to me. It was them. They told me to get in and I did. I know that sounds insane, but as my one sole focus was to get home, I thought they were my best bet. It was a massive risk but I couldn't see any other option. Besides I also knew I didn't really have a choice as I didn't have the energy or ability to fight them off anyway. They had already forced themselves on me; I wasn't sure how it could get any worse.

Unfortunately the half-hour drive back to High Wycombe was almost more traumatic than the rape itself. I was now much more mentally aware, and hearing the two men discuss the crime they had just committed against me broke my heart. I'll spare you the details of every dirty, disgusting thing they said as they sat there in front of me, laughing. It will stay with me forever though.

When I saw familiar roads and buildings, I wanted to cry with relief. The guys pulled up where I had been collected earlier that night, and I was grateful for the one bit of foresight I had shown in not giving them my actual address. They watched as I walked up a nearby alley, pretending that took me to my home. Once they had driven off I walked back, and along the road to my house.

I let myself in and ran a bath. A bath so hot I could barely stand to get in, but I needed to wash everything away. I climbed in and scrubbed every inch of my skin over and over again. I remember opening my vagina and trying to swirl as much water as possible inside me, trying to get rid of any residue or sign that those two vile, inhumane creatures had been inside of me. Did they use a condom? I don't even know.

It felt like something inside me had died. I knew I was never going to be the same again.

Mum knocked on the door and asked if I was OK. I must have woken her up, and I am sure she wondered what the hell I was doing, having a bath in the early hours of the morning. For a split second I thought about telling her the truth, but what was the point? She would want me to go to the police and I couldn't face that. All I wanted was to be left alone and to forget about everything.

So I took what seemed like the only route I could handle at the time.

'I'm fine,' I shouted back. As she headed back to bed I lay back in the cooling water, and began the systematic filing away of everything that had happened. Locking it away in the deepest recess of my mind with the hope I would never have to see or think about it again.

From then on, life changed. Two things in particular happened as a result of that night in 2006. First, the depression that had been hanging around in the background for most of my life began to play a bigger role, and second, I became very promiscuous.

In terms of depression I think I have probably suffered with it for most of my life. Looking back at my childhood and teen years I certainly showed all the signs of it, and I was going through the feelings and emotions that would have ticked all the boxes, but I just didn't know how to vocalise it.

I am certainly genetically disposed to it. I remember as a child seeing my uncle going off to be an in-patient at a mental hospital, and other members of my family followed suit at different points as I was growing up.

A lot of the time it was as though there was this huge empty sadness inside of me. I never felt as though I fitted in, as though I was good enough, as though I was able to be who I really am. There was this hole inside me that nothing ever seemed to fill. And I was always crying. Great, heaving, sobbing, end-of-the-world-type crying. It wasn't rare during my teenage years for me to have to take myself off to my bedroom at least once a day to let my emotions out in private.

If anyone ever mentioned my tears or sadness, they would put it down to hormones: 'Oh, you're a teenager, I guess it's to be expected.' But I knew it was something bigger, that I was sad in a way that I didn't feel my peers were. I just wasn't sure why.

In retrospect, suffering depression would also have been closely linked in to some of my other problems, such as self-harm and eating issues. Everything is so emotionally and physically tied in together when it comes to our brains.

But it was in this period of my life in college after the rape that I think the depression really began building up. I was self-harming, having a hard time over my weight, ongoing difficulty with teachers in college, and no matter how much I tried to keep it contained, this huge dark secret of the night in the university halls was eating me up from the inside out. I went to a sexual health clinic, worried about what one of the men could have passed on. Luckily I was given the all-clear, but I didn't tell the nurse what had happened or why I was worried. I didn't tell anyone at all. I didn't even acknowledge to myself what had happened. What was the point? This 'thing' needed to be locked away tightly for ever, if I was to get on with my life. At least that is what I thought at the time was the best way to deal with my shame and horror.

But ignoring what had happened was just contributing to my living hell – because no matter how much I convinced myself I was getting over it, the rape was like a confirmation of my worthless feelings, proof that all I was worthy of was being used by guys.

So where a lot of people react to rape by cutting themselves off from people – in particular, men – wearing no make-up or any clothes that could make them stand out, hiding away from social gatherings in case it draws attention to themselves, I went the other way. I would set out to get male attention, to make them look and take notice, then if they wanted sex I would go along with it. After all, men had got to decide what they could do with my body before, when I had had no say, so if they wanted it they got it, right? I know it was a self-destructive path, but it was the only way I knew how to cope at the time.

So for several months I was very promiscuous. I didn't set out to enjoy sex, and if I am being 100 per cent honest I couldn't even tell you half the people I had sex with or the things I did during that time. I was so numb, I think my mind was shut off from the outside world in a way. I was like a robot going through the motions, attempting to do anything to block out memories of the sexual assault, of being raped, of two strangers doing what they liked with me, while I had no choice.

I would use social media to find these guys. We would begin talking in a chat room and then we would agree to meet, but they were the most awful, self-destructive hook-ups. When they wanted sex it would boost my self-esteem and I would feel good – until after it had happened. Then I would feel like absolute shit, and be filled with guilt, shame and embarrassment. I think I had lost all concept of self-worth and self-respect, and constantly told myself: 'Grace, this is all you are good enough for.'

It only ended when I met a guy called Demi in one of the chat rooms and did actually like him, so we began dating properly. Then all my relationships with other men ended.

It was a year on from the sexual assault before I told anyone about it. I broke down one day and told a friend and she moment-arily convinced me I needed to report the boys to the police.

I was so worried about trying to put into words what had happened and knew that I could only give a broken report of the attack, thanks to whatever had been in my drink. I was also worried that people would be sure to find out and I would for-ever be known as 'that girl', and people would question why I had gone there in the first place. I also questioned whether I was at fault by going to their room alone – effectively going down the route of self-blame that sadly so many rape victims go through. All my doubts rapidly shut down the glimmer of hope my friend had given me. I decided the only thing I could do was carry on dealing with the assault the way I had been up until then – by doing my best to forget about it and trying to get on with life.

Through everything at least I still had dance. My beloved dance, that brilliant means of escape. I would throw myself into the routines and for a few moments, if all went well, my mind would think of nothing but the movements and the music. I would be happy.

When I was in a good place, it was like my love of the dance could drown out any negative voices or sadness. The performing and expression would make me come alive and allow me to feel truly free, at least for the short time I was doing it.

But if I was having a bad mental health day, I struggled a lot more with the negative voices in my mind, and dance didn't always win through.

One day at college we were doing pair work, and the teacher pulled me to one side and told me the next move in the routine involved lifts, but none of the boys would be able to pick me up as I was too heavy.

I have got rid of a lot of the photos of me at the time as I hated how I looked and I know I wasn't tiny, but I also wasn't this huge great elephant. I am going to guess I was about a size twelve, but combined with my height, OK, yes, I would not have been the lightest for someone to lift. But I was still really offended. Wouldn't you be? How about she tell the boys off for not having developed enough muscles to lift me? Lol! Or better yet, come up with a routine without lifts that we could all do. It really played on my mind, as yet again, here we were back to my weight. At a time when I was already depressed and feeling worthless, it did little to help.

As the course went on and everyone was discussing what they wanted to do next, I decided I wanted to go on to one of the London dance colleges. I auditioned for two and got in. But I couldn't put the teacher's voice out my head: 'You need to lose weight if you really want to be a dancer. You are too heavy for the boys to lift.' And my own repeated negativity: 'You are too fat, you will never make it. Everyone at stage school will laugh at you, and you will fail. You are one big fat failure.'

Combine that with all the other awful things that were going on in my head and I just wasn't strong enough to fight it. I turned down the places.

Other people's perceptions of weight, and my own body image demons had defeated the one thing in life that made me the happiest.

So while all my friends headed off to university or to study elsewhere, I stayed at home. I was still living with my mum, and couldn't see where my life was going. I was very confused about my future and although in some ways I wanted big things for myself and knew I needed to get out of my home town, I couldn't figure out how, or what I really wanted to do.

It didn't help that I wasn't getting on well with Mum or my sister by this stage. The days of the Three Musketeers were long gone, and I was living a very separate life from them, in my own angry, depressed world.

I was feeling lost and confused without my true friends – my stage school crew. I was left behind, alone, and it felt like it high-lighted the fact that I was the rubbish one. They were all taking their careers forward in the acting and dance world, and I could no longer compete. I had fallen by the wayside.

I suddenly felt very abandoned, and realised how much I had relied on them to keep me buoyed up and happy. They had known and understood the real me better than anyone else. But I never told them I felt lonely. I wasn't one for emotional chat with friends at that time, and instead I kept up the image of bubbly, positive Grace, loving life back home. Although I was scared, I was also embarrassed of those feelings, as I knew how babyish it would sound if I said it out loud, so I kept it to myself.

They never said that they missed me either, and who knows, maybe they didn't. I do think they were all a lot more practical about the route that life takes you, and maybe that was because they had much more stable upbringings and a grounded basis for their emotions. They followed the usual societal roles without question – school, college, uni – and the changes and movement of friends that went with it, without a second thought. For that I admired them, but for me, my safety net was gone. I struggled with it massively and wanted to keep my little friendship group, my bubble of attachment with them.

I am sure the whole thing probably tapped in to the general abandonment theme that had run through my life, from Dad, to the school bullies, to boyfriends. I realise at that age friends and boys do come and go, that friendship circles change and you date different boyfriends. But I always took every relationship end as a sign that I wasn't good enough, that people were moving on because they were fed up of me. I would take what were probably quite natural teenage transitions as something deeper, as a rejection of me.

So I started trying to find new friends. Social media became my window to the outside world for friends as well as hook-ups. I would come home from work, and get on to whatever chat room I preferred at the time, mostly Myspace or MSN, and chat to random people. It was my outlet and my way of dealing with things, but really it emphasised my loneliness. These girls weren't ever going to be my real friends, as I kept choosing really toxic people. I got sucked into this whole online world, and became even unhappier, as it wasn't providing me with what I was looking for.

Everything just kept piling in on top of me and actually many of my memories from the rape at the age of sixteen until I was twenty-one are quite a blur. I was in the depth of depression and feeling so unwell and unhappy that rather than memories, what I have is more a general sense of feeling sad, hating my body, hating my life, feeling trapped, isolated and completely worthless.

What is interesting though is that although I had times when I literally couldn't get out bed as I felt that bad, I was still very conscious of sending out an image to the rest of the world of the kind of person they expected me to be. Crazy! Bubbly! Confident! Funky! Loud! Sassy Grace!

I began getting lots of tattoos and piercings, and I think the idea was if I looked bright and colourful on the outside, people wouldn't know what was happening inside. They would assume the same old extroverted Grace that they had expected me to be all my life was still there.

Several years on, I am proud to say I found the inner strength to report my abusers.

As I became more confident in myself and began to recognise that mine is a body to be proud of, that it is MY body, and that no one should ever touch it without my permission, I could no longer suppress the memories of the rape, and became both angry and sad about it all over again.

I knew I needed to do something about it once and for all. On one level I needed to do it for my own peace of mind, to know that if there was a small chance those guys could be stopped from reoffending it was important that I take it. But also now that I was becoming a role model, the last thing I wanted to do was to give the message to other girls that they should let guys like that get away with their crimes. Hell, no. I wanted to lead by example.

So one day I picked up the phone and called the police. It felt surreal to give the factual details to this officer at the end of the phone.

I was shaking when I hung up, relieved that it had been such a simple process, sad that it had to happen, but also proud of myself. I had finally taken the step that part of me had desperately wanted to do over the years.

Everything I had to say is now in the police database, and I hope that if these vile men ever offend again or if it turns out they have done anything similar in the past, then this might match up to another brave girl's report and, combined with it, could help lead to a conviction.

In a perfect world I wish I had reported it at the time, and I would urge anyone who has gone through a similar experience and who feels able to do so, to get in touch with the police as soon as you can. But I wasn't mentally strong enough for it at the time, and the number one priority after a situation like this is to look after yourself, so I am not going to beat myself up about that any longer.

Now I am just glad I have come to love and respect my own body, and realise that it deserves nothing less than love and respect from anyone else.

Slut Shaming

I was slut shamed a lot in the period when I was being promiscuous and I think it is an issue that needs to be addressed. No one knew or understood why I was behaving the way I was, and I think that people need to realise that often if a young person is sleeping around there are underlying issues, often linked in with a lack of self-respect. But aside from that fact, it was none of their business anyway. It is not up to people to decide how many partners another person should have, and then make them feel like shit when it doesn't match up – whether because that figure is deemed too low or too high.

Growing up it didn't matter for boys how many people they had been with, but for girls in my area by the time of college, the magic number was three or four. Any less, you were frigid, any more and you were a slut. The perception was that too many partners meant you were no longer pure and sacred, as you had been touched by lots of different men.

Add this judgement to my rape, where I hadn't even con-sented to the sex, and I felt like damaged goods. I had a complex that I would never be fixed and no one would ever want me for sex again. That notion that I had somehow been ruined lasted a long, long time.

Now, it makes me really angry that anyone thinks they can set rules like that for someone to live by. But over time I had friends and ex-boyfriends call me a slut, and actually I have to hold my hands up, I have slut shamed people in my time too. It was an insult that everyone threw about when they really wanted to hurt someone. That was how women were treated and how they treated others, and I didn't know any differently.

As a result, what happened is everyone ended up lying: 'Oh yes, I'm completely innocent and pure, I've only had sex a few times.'

Note: Sorry to anyone who has ever dated or had sex with me, I probably lied to you about my 'number' . . . Oops!

Then, when people began talking about the double standards of our society and the hypocrisy of it, it got me thinking. I began to realise I shouldn't be ashamed of the choices I had made, as they were mine to make. The realisation was a nice feeling.

So now I know better, and I do better. Now I would never call anyone a slut. If a woman is sexually liberated and wants to do whatever she wants . . . that is her choice. For me personally I want to have sex with whoever I want, whenever I want, but I also don't want to have sex with just anyone. I want the options and to feel free, but I don't need to always use that right. I'll be my own judge of who is OK and not, I'll set the levels of my own self-respect, thank you very much!

Getting Support for Rape

Rape Crisis gives advice for women and girls who have been raped or experienced any other form of sexual violence at any time. Look on www.rapecrisis.org.uk to find your nearest centre, or call them for a chat on 0808 802 9999. Their advice for anyone who has just been raped is to get somewhere safe and warm, and talk to a friend or family member, or contact one of their centres. If you need urgent care or would like to instantly report the rape, call 999.

Chapter 6
WHEN I ACTUALLY TRIED TO DIE

'Sometimes you have to be broken to let the light in.'

The first time I tried to kill myself, I was twenty-one years old and at one of the darkest points of my life. Every day was a struggle, and I didn't feel I could cope any more. My mental health issues were at an all-time high, and I couldn't see a way past them. Every day was a battle to even get out of bed, and it was a huge achievement for me to shower or do my teeth. I literally could hardly even bring myself to speak.

My once wonderful relationship with Demi had now turned toxic, which didn't help, but it wasn't my boyfriend's fault; he just didn't know how to cope with me either. But as a result of his frustration and inability to understand what was happening, he was making things even worse for me.

I couldn't see a way out of it all, and would go round and round with darker and darker thoughts, and eventually I decided I had had enough. I took a whole bunch of sleeping pills, and went to sleep. I warned you this book might get heavy at times, sorry!

When I woke up the next morning, my first feeling was one of disappointment, 'Shit, I'm alive.' It was not the result I was after, and all I had to show for my suicide attempt was a sore head and stomach. There was no sense of relief about the fact that I was alive, I just felt hollow and gutted to still be here.

I didn't tell anyone what I had done, and a month later, I tried once more, again by overdosing on pills. I knocked them back one by one until I lost count of how many I had taken, and fell asleep. Again it didn't work, I just ended up with a horrible few days feeling drowsy, suffering from a banging headache, and unable to keep any food down. It was all just one big fat mess – I couldn't do anything right, I couldn't even manage to kill myself properly.

Today I am obviously massively relieved that I didn't succeed. There was far too much living still to do. And actually, let's face it, there must have been a bit of me that didn't want to die. If I had been really determined to end my life, I could easily have researched the necessary number of pills and made sure I counted them out so I was good to go. But I didn't.

I think the reality was I was suffering really badly from depression, my mental health was all over the place, and it was a cry for help of sorts, as I just couldn't see any way out of it. It felt like I was in a big fat downward spiral with no light at the end of the tunnel.

I kept thinking I was coping with everything in life, that the best way to deal with all my problems was to box them off, ignore them, and move on from them. But it was clear from my behaviour that it wasn't working, and all the signs were pointing to the fact my mind was in a really bad place.

I am sure my situation wasn't helped by my job at the time. I was in an awful office-based job that was all focused on numbers and data inputting. Oh my God, it was soul destroying. I didn't see daylight from one hour to the next, the air was this horrible fake air-con stuff, and I was just sitting at a desk with no chance to mix with other people or be creative. Everything was all about office politics and real petty shit. I didn't like one thing about that job, from the tasks to the bosses to my colleagues to the environment it was in, and I was desperately unhappy. All I wanted to do was dance but my self-esteem was so low that I didn't believe I could do it. I was allowing my mental health issues to hold me back from doing what I loved.

As my mental health got worse, I began binge eating to get through the day, and my weight shot up. Apart from dragging myself to the office I was hardly leaving bed or communicating with anyone. It was a good day if I managed to wash and get out of my pyjamas, and I couldn't bring myself to cook, so it was all about ready meals, take-outs and snacks.

It felt like everything was falling apart and depression kicked in with a vengeance. I had managed to suppress all my problems from the previous years while it felt like I had a focus in life and daily tasks that kept my mind and body busy. But it was as if working in this office opened that all back up again. And of course, as with all these self-destructive cycles, when one thing goes wrong it has a knock-on effect. The more I hated work, the more I took it out on my boyfriend and the more messed-up our relationship became, then the more that added to my unhappiness. Day-to-day functioning just began to feel like too much effort, and not something I wanted to be bothered with.

After my second suicide attempt, instead of trying again, I asked for help. I didn't wait for someone else to take responsibility, I sat up and did it myself. It took everything in me to do so, but despite all my problems it was clear there was a part of me that wanted to live. Deep down inside me was a will to fight back, and for whatever reason it came to the surface. I knew I desperately needed to act in some way to end this horrible downward spiral. Who knows, maybe there was a way out of it, even if it didn't feel that way at the time. So I called my doctors' surgery. I was terrified, embarrassed and ashamed but I knew I needed to act. 'There is something wrong with me,' I told the receptionist. 'I need help.'

They got me down to the surgery and I had to fill out forms answering questions about my feelings and experiences. It was a real effort for once to write the truth, rather than what I thought people wanted to hear. The doctor talked to me about my options and I agreed that I should start counselling. We decided that talking about what I was going through rather than taking medication of any sort was the way forward, and he referred me for treatment at Haleacre, a mental health unit in Amersham.

That was just before Christmas 2011, and I somehow managed to get through the next couple of months until I began therapy in February 2012. I don't remember how I did it; I think it was just a case of existing, getting through each day at a time. Waiting and surviving, and living off the bit of hope that therapy might help me deal with the mess in my mind.

Everyone needs a different type of treatment, depending on what the causes are for what you are going through, and what you react to. For me they thought it would be a combination of CBT (cognitive behavioural therapy) and counselling. I didn't like the CBT side of it, as it just didn't really make sense to me. I would always be wondering what it had to do with anything, and I was given homework and little tasks to do at home to make myself feel better that just felt stupid. Maybe it wasn't the right treatment for me, or maybe I just wasn't open to it at the time, I'm not sure. I know I definitely wasn't open to the idea of the group sessions they booked me in for. At the last minute I refused to go, as the idea of sharing my problems with a room full of strangers just seemed too terrifying. Counselling was the treatment that suited me best.

Key Therapies

- **Counselling:** Basically, this means talking therapy. Chatting through a situation or problem to get to the root of it and see how it can be dealt with.

- **CBT:** This looks at the way you view yourself and the world, and helps you to respond more positively. The aim is to get out of destructive patterns of thought or behaviour in 'the now' rather than looking at causes and symptoms.

- **Psychotherapy:** This focuses more on your past, and dealing with and processing certain events within it, as well as the way they have impacted on your present.

- **Group therapy:** Around twelve people dealing with similar problems meet to discuss them. It works well in giving you support and making you realise you aren't the only person going through difficulties.

It didn't take long for my counsellor in the one-on-one sessions to diagnose me as having body image issues, anxiety and depression. The diagnosis was actually a relief to hear. It was like, OK, something actually is wrong, I have a mental health disorder, it is not just all in my mind, I am not going crazy. It was helpful in a sense to have that confirmation, as I instantly then thought, right, well I can move forward and get better now.

I would go to a day session every week. My therapist touched on the fact she thought some of the issues might stem from me feeling abandoned by my dad and we talked about his input – or lack of it – in my childhood. It was the first time anyone had suggested that his behaviour could be at the root of my issues. Although it did ring true, we didn't go into it in too much depth, but it was something I would revisit later.

Instead we ended up focusing on my weight, which, as ever, was a massive issue for me. I had ballooned from eating the same diet I had been eating while bulimic, but now I was no longer making myself sick. We discussed body image and ways to tackle it, including actually losing the weight.

In terms of the anxiety diagnosis, I knew I was scared or worried about certain situations but I hadn't realised it was anxiety. I don't suffer from anxiety in day-to-day situations, like people who hate travelling, or get claustrophobic. Scenarios like that are fine for me; it is much more about the emotional associations of a situation. Ironically, although I hadn't been convinced by the diagnosis at the time, this is an aspect of my mental health that has got worse as I have got older. I now recognise that I get anxious if I feel I am starting to lose control of my life. If I am so busy with work and commitments that I end up cancelling a meeting with a friend or a doctor's appointment, I feel as though I am losing control, and that fuels my anxiety.

When I am suffering from anxiety, it affects my whole body. The physical and the mental are so closely linked that I end up feeling drained and my skin will come out in spots. I also have to run to the toilet all the time with diarrhoea. Is that TMI? But 'anxiety diarrhoea' is a genuinely recognised medical condition, I promise you! When you are anxious, adrenalin kicks in, and apparently that messes with the distribution of liquids in your body, including within your bowels.

So how did I deal with it?

Well, let me start by saying that I am not a doctor or trained therapist; I am just a girl who has 'been there done that' with far too many mental health problems. And although I will tell you shortly about the training I have done in this area, I am obviously just telling you my own thoughts and experiences. You need to decide what works best for you, or see a doctor if necessary. (I guess this is my disclaimer of sorts!)

I have learnt to deal with anxiety by focusing on breathing. The more your body is not being regulated by air, the worse a state you get into, and the more the anxiety kicks in. I always try and do ten deep breaths, counting them in and out slowly. Sometimes I don't even realise how quickly I am breathing when I am anxious until I sit down and think about it, and once I have it under control it helps to calm me.

Interestingly, there is a link between breathing and food and drink, and the way that people can turn to food or drink when anxious, whether that is a cup of coffee or a chocolate bar. When you eat, it regulates your breathing. Think about it next time you sit down for a meal. You are forced to breathe in a calm, measured way, to fit it around each mouthful, so if you are feeling anxious, this can settle you down.

If people don't realise that it is the breathing calming them they can start to believe that it is the food itself that is making them feel better, which can lead to an anxious person turning to food all the time. It can become almost an addiction, a medication to soothe them, which they associate with feeling good. Over time they can end up turning to food for comfort, even when they are not stressed. This explains why so many people who are prone to anxiety put on weight, and why eating disorders can be linked to other mental health problems. I have often wondered if this was part of the reason for my weight gain when I was younger.

Panic Attacks

For as long as I can remember I have known what a panic attack is, but fucking hell, that knowledge didn't make it any easier the first time I had one. I felt as if I couldn't breathe and was going to die and it was one of the most real and horrific sensations I have ever experienced.

I have had four full-blown panic attacks in my life, and that has been four too many. Each time I have been crying, hot, flustered and unable to breathe. One time I kind of half blacked out and thought someone had turned all the lights out. I was screaming for someone to turn them on, when the room was apparently still fully lit.

The sensation after a panic attack is bizarre, too. I feel a bit sick, achy and tired, but I also feel calm and serene, like a storm has passed.

The reason for the panic attacks in my case has always been a trauma of sorts – splitting up with a boyfriend, a vicious falling out with a friend, or a particularly traumatic counselling session. Clearly, dealing with particularly emotional issues is what fuels the panic attack for me, as though my body is tied in to my mental state, and is trying to come to terms with what has happened to me.

The breathing that I learnt to use to deal with anxiety also worked with panic attacks. It is a key technique for me with most stressful situations really. Any time I am very stressed or unhappy, I can almost guarantee that my breathing will be out of sync, and pulling it back in can go a long way to improving things. I use an app called Breathe2Relax on my phone that has a picture of a guy breathing in and out, or up and down to get your diaphragm involved, and the idea is to follow it. Taking deep breaths along with the app can really slow down my breathing and pull me back to a good place.

Apart from the diagnosis and reassurance that I wasn't alone, I am not sure the treatment I got the first time was that effective. Looking back, the counsellor touched on issues that were clearly at the root of much of what I was going through, and that made me aware of some of the problems. But we didn't delve into them or tackle them deeply; it was very much a surface sweep of everything. So it was like I became aware of the existence of these feelings and problems I had filed away in boxes in the back of my brain, but we never actually opened them up or dealt with them.

Having said that, I can't knock it too much either, as it basically saved my life. Without being referred to that centre and being given the knowledge that someone was listening to me and understood me on some level, I am not sure I would ever have begun to deal with my mental health issues, and I may well have slipped back down a suicidal path again.

I think, looking back, perhaps I was suppressing so many of the problems that the counsellor struggled to get out of me. My attitude – wrongly – was very much that I had my diagnosis, so that was practically me better, now I wanted to get on with life.

I do believe everyone would benefit from seeing a counsellor or a therapist at least once in their life. Every single one of us needs to unload our problems at some point, and will have issues in our lives that we are struggling to deal with. Bottling everything up is never good, and often getting a fresh perspective or opinion can make the problem instantly seem smaller.

The majority of us talk to friends and family, and that is great, but there is also a limit as to how helpful that can be. In some situations those closest to us may not have the knowledge to link certain behaviour patterns to incidents and traumas, and in others they may be too close to you or the event to give genuine unbiased help.

Then of course you need to consider them, and the impact your unburdening could have on them. Ultimately they may end up holding your burden as well as their own, and that is not fair on a person's mental capacity, if they are not trained for it.

There is an important issue to be aware of called emotional contagion. This means that whenever you tell anyone anything, positive or negative, they take on some of the feeling. So say I tell you a really good, uplifting story, you will leave our conversation feeling happy and empowered. If I tell you a sad story, it can put you in a sad, depressed place. This can also occur when discussing our problems, and so that we don't all end up carrying each other's shit around, we should make use of trained professionals. This is particularly relevant if you have suffered with trauma, and a lot of people have, whether you recognise it as that or not.

Of course that is not to say you shouldn't talk to friends and family – sharing feelings with them is a very important part in a person's journey of recovery. I just think it is important that if things have got very bad, friends and family are *part* of the support network, not all of it.

How Common are Mental Health Problems?

According to the charity Mind (mind.org.uk), the most recent survey done in England on mental health was in 2009 and concluded that out of 100 people, this many suffered from the following problems:

- Depression: 2.6
- Anxiety: 4.7
- Mixed anxiety and depression: 9.7
- Phobias: 2.6
- OCD: 1.2
- Panic disorder: 1.2
- Post-traumatic stress disorder: 3
- Eating disorders: 1.6

That is just one year, so you can imagine over a lifetime. This is not an issue that can be ignored. It impacts on us all, or someone we know.

Mental health sadly is still quite a taboo topic. It is so desperately important, and yet still not talked about with ease. It is more important than any other type of health as your brain is crucial to your wellbeing – obviously. It is where your emotions and happiness come from. It needs to be discussed in a much more open manner by everyone in society, and we should all have a better understanding of how to deal with someone who is going through it. The upside is that it is coming out into the open more and more all the time and I hope blogs and vlogs such as mine are helping people with that.

One thing that makes me sad about this period of my life, and it is quite hard to admit this, is that it felt that not one person ever seemed to think there was anything wrong with me, or that I might need to have, or get, some help. I mean my family and my boyfriend could tell I was unhappy and things were not going well, but they either didn't know how to tackle it, or didn't think it was worth doing so. I tried to tell them a few times just how bad I was feeling, but it always felt as though it was brushed aside. No one ever went, 'Wow, OK, we need to get this girl some help,' or even just said to me, 'OK, we can see things are bad, what can we do to make you feel better about yourself?'

For someone who was already feeling in such a negative place, it was as though they didn't give a shit. That they didn't really care if I was dead or alive. I know that wasn't the case, but again the overwhelming idea that I was unloved and not good enough was the overriding force in my thought process.

In retrospect, I think they actually just didn't know what to do. Mental health was not something that was really discussed where I grew up. You pulled yourself together and cracked on with life, and that was it.

Now I know that the best thing to do if you suspect someone is going through this is check they are alright, let them know you are there for them, and offer your time. Maybe they will want to talk, maybe they won't, but at least they won't feel alone. If you find it difficult to approach the topic of mental health, leave some leaflets and information out for them, and make it as easy as possible for them to ask for help.

At the time though I think my family just thought I was being dramatic or weak. Or if they did suspect something deeper, they didn't know how to broach the subject, so it was easier to just brush it under the carpet.

Except for me that wasn't the easier route. It is what I was trying to do, but it just meant I kept my feelings and very dark thoughts all closed up and festering, and eventually that was going to have consequences.

How to See a Counsellor

- The first port of call is generally your doctor. Yes, it takes some real courage to make that phone call, but take a deep breath and go for it. Remember, the receptionists hear all sorts, all day long, and are trained to deal with people, while keeping everything confidential. If it helps and you have someone you have confided in, such as a friend or family member, they could do that initial call for you.

- It is rare that you find the perfect therapist or type of therapy for you on the first try. Think of it like everything else in life; it can take some research, experimentation, and trial and error.

The first foundation you try, first dress you pick off the rails . . . it is very lucky you get the perfect one first time! I hadn't really understood this on my first experience or I would have looked at other options, and that is very important to remember. Give the therapist and their methods a good try, but if they aren't for you, move on, go through the process again, until you find that person who really can help you.

- There is of course the private option, and I did try this down the line, as you will see. My experience of it was much better, but I obviously can't say that would be the same in all cases. Of course it costs, and in certain cases and clinics, can cost a lot. But if you have the finances and are willing to invest, it is definitely an option to look into.

Useful Numbers

- **Samaritans:** This is a UK charity that offers emotional support to people feeling suicidal, distressed, or struggling to cope. You can chat anonymously, twenty-four hours a day, 365 days of the year. Call them on 116 123 or email jo@samaritans.org. There are also local branches where you can drop in for a chat. See more at www.samaritans.org.

- **Mind:** The guys at Mind have created a real hub of information on practically any area of mental health that you can think of. They also offer support. See www.mind.org.uk or phone 0300 123 3393.

- **It's Good to Talk:** The website helps find private counsellors and psychotherapists in your area, and gives contact details and prices. There is also information on the different types of therapy, how they work, and how to tell which one might be the best for you. See www.itsgoodtotalk.org.uk.

Chapter 7
TURN YOUR PAIN INTO PASSION

'Do sharks complain about Mondays? No! They are up early biting shit, chasing stuff, being scary. This is your reminder that you are a shark!'

So I guess one thing you lovely lot will want to know is how I actually got into YouTube and making the kind of videos that I do in the first place. For that we'll have to rewind a few years . . .

While everything had been going wrong in my life while I was in college, I had found one amazing and incredible place that had gone some way to rebalance the awfulness.

I was seventeen, hanging out round the streets and parks, drinking Lambrini straight from the bottle, kissing random boys and getting in cars with people I had just met, when a friend introduced me to a couple called Jay and Jade. They were running youth clubs around the town under the name Street Dreams, and would visit areas where they knew kids like me were hanging out so they could talk to us. I warmed to them straight away as they were honest and friendly and didn't talk down to us, so I agreed to go along to the club with some friends.

They were a charity who, in their own words, acted 'as an extended family to disadvantaged, disengaged and disruptive young people to help them achieve a sustainable, positive life. The main aim is to motivate and elevate young people so that the community becomes a better place to live in.'

They were creating these safe havens around Bucks for people to hang out in, and I went to one at a venue called Roundhouse. It was full of kids from all sorts of backgrounds, cultures and races, although it had a very urban feel and the majority were ethnic minorities from poorer backgrounds and the council estates.

The youth club was our safe place, where we could dance, sing, play basketball and generally hang out. Jay and Jade provided food for us, really fresh home-cooked warm food that did the world of good for a bunch of teenagers who were living off fast food and junk. I loved spending time there, and in a way it felt like we were one big ridiculous family.

When I left college at eighteen and wasn't sure what to do next, Jade offered me a job with Street Dreams. That was what they did best – bring in kids, give them hope and a reason to live, then continue looking out for them even after they reached their adult years.

There were many sides to my role, and I got a huge kick out of it. There was the office-based side of things where I learnt about admin, expenses and receipts, petty cash, income and outgoings. I also became more adept with editing photos, filming and areas like advertising. But it was the practical side I really enjoyed. I would help out at the youth clubs doing music sessions with up-and-coming rappers, grime artists and MCs. There was a kids' club at a nearby women's refuge that tried to give the kids a sense of normality and focus, so I would go there and teach them to dance. I worked with some kids who had been kicked out of school and talked to them about topics that they wanted to know about, but didn't have a role model to discuss things with, such as sex. It was like I was getting the best of so many different worlds: the youth club I had loved, the adult world of responsibility, the chance to keep on dancing while earning reasonable money. I was loving it, and realised I had quite a passion for teaching and helping people be the best they could be. I thrived off every daily challenge, and felt like I had found my goal in life. I also felt like I was the richest person in the world, taking home a whole £908 a month!

Jay and Jade were fantastic, and were my first real role models in terms of leading by example to show me the person I could be and the differences I could make. Jay was the first really positive black role model in my life. A black man who was good, kind, successful, kept his life on the straight and narrow, and was respectful to others.

Then there was his relationship with his wife Jade, who was Turkish. They were the first mixed-race couple I had seen who were so happy together, and had a really strong bond. I looked at them as a second mum and dad, and even called them that. It wasn't just what they stood for that inspired me though, it was that they put their money where their mouth was, and helped me actually go down the road to being more like them. When they took me in to work for them they gave me the fuel and the knowledge to work in a field that helped others, and drew out of me that desire to work with troubled and disadvantaged people. Without them I wouldn't be where I am today. Their whole ethos was so empowering and positive, and encouraged everyone to develop as individuals. They showed me what you can do with your life, and set me on the right track.

I can honestly say working with them was the first time I really believed that you could succeed in whatever way you wanted to, without being middle class, skinny and white.

Then suddenly one day Street Dreams lost funding and could no longer afford to hire staff. My first great job was over. It had been a brilliant first experience of a full-time job, so I was really sorry at the news, both for myself and Street Dreams, who shortly after had to completely close as they could no longer function without being able to employ helpers.

I had been doing the job for a year by then, and the money was good enough to get by, but I hadn't been saving anything, so I needed to get another job real quick. I had been paying rent to my mum towards the family home, bills, food etc., and she couldn't afford to have me there if I wasn't able to contribute. I went on Jobseeker's Allowance but decided I couldn't afford to be fussy, and would take the first half-decent job that came along. That is how I ended up in that horrific office admin job ...

I think one of the reasons that I got into watching YouTube videos to pass the time in the evenings was because I was so bored and unhappy in my job. They provided a great distraction from the dull, tedious day I had just had and it was exciting to see how everyone else was living their life. The way everyone talked was calm, happy and whimsical, and the most difficult or controversial topic covered would be something like whether blue eye shadow was ever acceptable. That was fine for me at the time, though. I have been interested in make-up ever since that day at school when I was thirteen and started experimenting with eye shadow, and fashion had long been a way for me to express myself. So I liked to see what other people had to say, even if I didn't always agree with them. As my depression developed and I rarely left the house, I became more and more reliant on these videos for a connection with other people and the outside world.

One thing I noticed was every single British person on it was white, middle-class, well-spoken and skinny. There were mixed-race girls with curly hair and curves vlogging in the US, but none in the UK, and I felt that was a bit of a gap in the market. I wanted to watch someone looking at make-up for mixed-race skin, clothes for curvy girls, and products for curly hair.

Then one day I decided I would make a few of my own videos about fashion and beauty – at the time that or gaming was all anyone really talked about on YouTube, so I didn't think I could veer away from that. I didn't have huge plans for it; I just thought it would be fun, and if I enjoyed it, I would keep it up as a hobby. So I set up an account, and called myself the 'Ugly Face of Beauty'. The name was a nod to the fact I had always considered myself to be ugly, but that over time I had explored the different sides of beauty, and the power that make-up, hairstyles and fashion can have in making you feel beautiful. I didn't know at that stage that the name would end up having even deeper relevance as my content grew and developed – unless my subconscious somehow knew . . . !

Anyhow that day I got all my make-up together – mainly MAC at the time – and sat in front of my shitty computer screen on my twenty-first birthday, and made a video of 'What's in my make-up bag'. All I wanted to do was make a video that someone like me would want to watch. My God, I rewatched it recently, and it is proper cringe. I was putting on this really posh voice, and the computer was such bad quality that whenever I moved my arm it was like it was going slow motion through the air, leaving a trail. And I can't even discuss the state of my eyebrows . . . But before any of you go looking for it, I have changed the settings to private, so you won't be able to find it!

But despite all of that, I really enjoyed making it, and even though no one else wanted me to do it – my boyfriend at the time told me it was pointless and would just embarrass me – I pushed ahead with it. Well, look at me now, mate! Ha!

No, it was actually a big deal for a different reason. I was so unhappy and unmotivated that having something that did interest me, that I could put my energies into, was a very important thing. I have learnt since that if you have mental health problems, having a creative outlet can be a massive part of recovery for a lot of people. For me that creativity was YouTube and blogging, and as always when there was a camera I was able to pretend I was someone else, so it wasn't too hard to put on a brave face and smile, even if it was not how I was feeling inside.

It was two years into the horrific office job, and several months after I began YouTube, that I hit rock bottom and attempted suicide. Thankfully, as we know, it was at that point that I started counselling, but I was in no position to be working and would have been a rubbish employee, so I took redundancy. I decided instead to focus on the counselling and my YouTube channel, which I was actually really enjoying. It was providing me with my one focal point and pleasure of the day. Not that it was of any use at all financially at this stage. I think I was earning £200 every few months or so from advertising, which just about allowed me to pay Mum a bit towards rent and bills.

Initially I went on Jobseeker's Allowance, but after a couple of months, as I began to feel a bit better, I started to think I needed to get back out there to work (and my bank balance was telling me the same). I was still due to be in therapy for another good while, but I decided that could run alongside work. I started looking around, and came across an advert for the role of a care assistant in a children's home. It described how I would be helping to look after kids with emotional and behavioural problems. Of course I had read Jacqueline Wilson's book *The Story of Tracy Beaker*, and watched it when it became a BBC show, but I thought that was fiction – surely children's homes didn't actually exist? At the time I thought foster parents were the only real option for social services when moving children. But I looked into the job, and I actually liked the sound of it. It had similarities to my role at Street Dreams with Jay and Jade, but was a step up from it, so I applied.

I was invited for interview, and bossed it of course! I was really proud of how well I did with the questions, and they said I was good, but then . . . I didn't hear from them for three months. I expected it to be a slow process as they explained there would be a lot of checks as the job was with very vulnerable children, but I was beginning to give up hope when I finally got a call. The job was mine. I was ecstatic.

It was May 2012 when I started the job and there were eight four-bedroom houses under our catchment. My lovely aunt Debbie had helped me out by buying me a car by then, so I was able to get to work in the first place.

The kids were between eleven and seventeen years old, although the majority were fourteen to sixteen. Our role was to give them love, care, safety and food, and make their lives as normal as possible. So on a typical day that might mean helping them sort out a new bus pass, taking them to the doctor or dentist, cooking them dinner, getting them to school on time, and telling them off when they were little shits! (Little shits who I still miss every day) It also meant helping them to relax safely and have positive, normal downtime, so I might watch TV with them, go bowling, to the cinema, swimming, or we would play games. Basically I had to help them live a normal life in a way they may never have had the chance to do before. It felt like a kind of dysfunctional extended family.

We were a team of fourteen and we all had our roles – there was the person who was like the mum, another like the gran. I was the cool older sister to the four kids in the house, and in a way I saw myself as a slightly older, more experienced version of them, so it was a role I fell into without much effort.

Most children will naturally trust parents and teachers, but children in care are often a lot more suspicious. They tend to know who is real and who is not, and I like to think they knew I was, and that was why I was able to build good relationships with them quickly.

I loved that job straight away. Every day was such a challenge.

It taught me to be patient but also to be strong, resilient, and have the courage and self-belief to tackle any problem.

After three months, my probation period was up. My weak points were swearing too much around the kids – if you don't want them to swear, you can't swear yourself. Also I wasn't so great at cleaning, as I hated it! I had smashed through everything else though, so I was kept on, having passed with flying colours.

Part way through my time there I got a new boss, a lady called Michelle Humphries, who is an incredible person who completely changed my life. She encouraged me and pushed me to be better all the time and gave me the platform on which to grow and develop. She also understood me and how my mind ticks, and gave me the confidence and expertise to handle most things in life.

I wanted to excel at my job, so as well as all the mandatory training, I put myself through all the optional courses as well. These could be anything from half-day to two-week courses, as the idea was I would pull it all together eventually for an NVQ, which would allow me to work across children's homes, schools and nurseries. I did training in:

- **Safeguarding children:** This covered everything from ensuring electrical wires weren't left lying around to teaching children how to keep themselves safe, and linking in with school to ensure they were safe there too. There were some dark areas that fell under this category too, such as sexual exploitation and how to cut someone down who is trying to hang themselves with a rope.

- **Emotional and behavioural training:** This means understanding the wellbeing of a child in your care and learning to manage their behaviour, which could be anything from mild anger to sexualised behaviour.
- **Physical restraints:** So basically how to stop a child if they got into a fight, or were lashing out.
- **Positive handling:** This is the step before physical restraint, so trying to calm a child before they go into crisis, whether that is removing them from the situation by guiding them out of the door, or trying to humour them away from the situation.
- **Attachment theory:** This is about dealing with a child with attachment problems. The idea is that from zero to three you develop a large part of your character, and how you are dealt with when you are screaming and crying as a toddler can influence your attachment levels later in life. For example, if your mum always goes to you, you are going to be heavily dependent on her while growing up. If she never comes to you, you may not develop a good sense of attachment with her, and struggle to achieve it with others. A healthy balance is ideal, but often children in care have a skewed idea of this.
- **Medication:** So how to take meds correctly, for example three times a day does not mean at breakfast, lunch and dinner, but every eight hours. How to hand out the medications and inject where necessary.
- **Drug and alcohol awareness:** Knowing the law and legislation around alcohol and drugs, as well as how to spot potential problems and tackle them.
- **Therapeutic care:** So the different language you would use to make it a therapeutic setting.

- **Self-harm:** How to recognise the signs in someone, and techniques for recovery from it.

Going on the last of those courses was understandably weird, but in a good way. Hearing other people's stories and really understanding why people do it actually helped me deal with my own self-harm issues. Self-harm is such a personal, private thing to do, that hearing other people's stories and experiences, as well as explanations of the psychology behind it, was a real eye-opener.

The course was run by this incredible woman who had adopted fifteen different children over the years, eight of whom were severe self-harmers. And by severe I mean on a whole other level than I had ever known existed. They would cut huge 10-inch long deep cuts into themselves, then rub soil into the wound or pour bleach over them. Others were smashing their heads with concrete, anything that would inflict maximum pain and damage. I had never heard it so bad.

One thing that interested me was that many of the courses were quite reactive, in that they would come in at the same time as a new law, or when there had been a serious case review. We did one that focused on the awful death of Baby P, who was tortured, abused and killed by his mother's boyfriend. This linked into the death of Victoria Climbié, who was killed by her great-aunt several years before, as both happened in the same London borough, so there were questions over whether it could have been prevented by the child protection services. We would go through these horrific scenarios and try to work out what went wrong, and what could have been done better.

More than anything it was time on the 'shop floor' that really mattered. Nothing beat the learning you got from dealing directly with the children, as while the training was so useful, you needed to be putting it into action. Besides, every child is so unique that sometimes you might find they don't respond to any positive handling techniques you have learnt and you have to think on your feet and work out the right way for yourself.

Experience and passion are the two things that I believe make for a really good worker in the children's home.

I found my forte was being the key person in the home for the girls and boys to talk to about sex. As I was so open about it, there was nothing they couldn't come and ask me or discuss with me.

At one point I worked with some of the kids who had been sex trafficked, which was just so difficult. But the support system in the home was great, and Michelle was my support assistant at that time, and really encouraged me through it.

CSE (child sex exploitation) is so damaging and horrific for any teenager that I think a lot more needs to be done to tackle it. Having been taken of advantage of myself, then trained in the area so that I could work with kids going through it, I would really like to raise more awareness of it. Over time I hope to do a documentary on it, and discuss it more on my channel, although the issue is so hard-hitting, I need to find the perfect way to do so.

I became a key worker, meaning I worked closely with one specific child who needed one-to-one help. Then I became a team leader, leading a whole shift. As the youngest person there in charge of people aged up to fifty years old, it was quite a responsibility, and a confidence boost to be trusted in this capacity. I basically got better and better, and really wanted to be good. I loved the challenges the job brought on a daily basis, and was becoming a person I was proud to be.

Don't get me wrong, though, there were a lot of difficult times, and I don't just mean the cleaning! No, there were sleepless nights – sleepless weeks even. I had my car smashed up, I was verbally and physically abused – punched in the face, spoken to like rubbish, slapped, spat at, pissed on, etc. But I think I took a lot of that in my stride, as I saw myself in a lot of the kids. They would display certain behaviour traits that I could identify with, or I would be able to see the root cause of it when no one else could, and understand why they were lashing out rather than dealing with it. But my God, the girls were the worst.

I was still going through therapy out of work, and although my mental health was improving a fair bit, I was still quite vulnerable, and so at times was signed off sick with stress. Having said that, the main cause wasn't my own problems, or because of any of those attacks, but more because I had become so attached to my amazing, dysfunctional little kids, and I was so desperate for them to see the world as I had learnt to see it, in particular the poor girls who had been exploited. I understood from my own experiences exactly what abuse was and what it felt like for your body to be treated like a commodity. But some of these girls couldn't see that their own treatment was wrong and abusive, they struggled to see their own self-worth, and I found that really, really hard.

But I always had Michelle to turn to for advice, and over time I felt she really helped me make a difference to these kids' lives. Michelle was a huge influence on my life in other ways too. She would talk to me about mental health in general, and showed me that the same way you could nurture a child, you can nurture yourself. She became one of my key role models in life, and I am still friends with her now and call her my aunt.

She once said to me: 'Each person chooses their own destiny and is either a victim or a survivor. You, Grace, are a survivor.' It really resonated with me as I kind of knew I was, but I didn't know how to say it, and she had articulated it perfectly. It was also a good kick up the arse to start acting like I was a survivor, too!

At the same time, it was dawning on me that despite all my flaws, I was becoming a good role model to these kids. I was instilling them with confidence and self-belief, an understanding of the world outside their small bubble, and a desire to be something more than they were, and to not be labelled by what they had been through.

I am still in touch with most of the kids, and recently one of them messaged me to say: 'I felt that you were really there for me, you felt like an older sister, always giving good advice, and guiding us down the right path.'

That touched me, and was exactly how I wanted them to think of me. It also made me realise how badly I had needed someone like me when I was a young teenager, to help get me on the right road.

If you are considering a career like this, you should know that you don't need many qualifications to work with kids in care as you get all the training when you start. However, I can't emphasise enough that it is not a field of work you can go into lightly. You need a passion for helping people and a real drive and hunger to be something positive in a child's life. The job isn't easy but for the right person it is *so* incredibly rewarding.

A Two-Way Relationship

My relationship with the kids was a two-way thing. Yes, I was there for them, looked after them, listened to them and was responsible for them, but actually they did the same for me, and helped form me into the person I am today.

So to those amazing kids: thank you for teaching me patience, strength, resilience and survival. Thank you for showing me that there is life after trauma, abuse and pain. Thank you for making me laugh, making me cry and keeping me up at night (when you little shits refused to go to bed). The late nights were the nights when I understood you the most. The nights when you showed me how vulnerable you are, despite the façade you would put on during the day. Thank you for Chinese takeaways and movie nights. Thank you for knowing when I wasn't OK and making me cups of squash. Thank you for allowing me to care for you. Thank you for recognising that I was genuine, when so many others had let you down. Thank you for believing in me and giving me the confidence and knowledge to do what I do now.

While all this was happening I was spending more and more time on my YouTube channel. I was loving learning how to do everything, and having an excuse to explore different make-up, fashions and hair products. But more than anything I was getting a kick out of the interaction with my followers. I felt like I had all these virtual friends and people with shared interests to talk to from the comfort of my own sofa. Maybe it played into the intro-verted extrovert part of me – I wanted the human contact and to be able to perform on some level, but at the same time I wanted to be hidden away in my own space.

My audience was growing despite the fact that I worried about being different to all the other vloggers. There I was with my big hair, freckles, ridiculous laugh that sounds like Adele's (if you have never heard her laugh, you have to Google it ...) and my potty mouth, all reflecting my very urban roots.

I was getting a good response from my viewers who often said they liked that I wasn't just this skinny, posh, blonde girl, but that I looked at clothes and make-up for a different kind of hair, skin colour and body shape. It seemed I was filling that gap in the market I had noticed, and I hadn't been the only one who wanted to watch someone more like me. I was trying to make it clear that it didn't matter who you were, you could still have a lot of fun making yourself look good, and that everyone had their own style and techniques that worked for themselves.

I began getting emails and messages telling me that I was a real inspiration to people, and thanking me for showing that you could be different, but still dress well, have fun and look good. People were happy that I was showing them tricks for big curly hair, that I was showcasing high-street clothes for larger girls, and that I wasn't just recommending expensive make-up or a ridiculous skin care routine.

The only problem was, it felt like this bubbly, larger-than-life character I was playing behind the camera – one who had no insecurities, was happy with the way she looked, and was living life without a care in the world – was basically a massive lie. No one knew I was in treatment, dealing with depression, body image issues and anxiety, or that I was going through eating problems, abandonment issues, battling self-harm, and all sorts of other shit. I worried that I was being hypocritical and fake, and it played on my mind more and more that no one really knew what was happening behind closed doors. Of course I was entitled to my private life, but I have always tried to be as real as I can be. If I wasn't, was I just creating yet another false perception that was doing nothing to help young people?

At the time I had no real direction planned out for my channel, I was just enjoying doing it, although I had begun to wonder if there was a more long-term career in it. Although I still was earning pennies from it, I could see other channels growing and starting to cash in.

I began getting invited to vlogging events, where it was the same small community of YouTubers at every event. We had found something in vlogging and in each other that we could all relate to, but at the same time I did stand out as I was very different to them all, in terms of appearance and background. Over time it has actually been good for me to stand out, but at the time I do think it meant I needed to have more self-belief and determination to be sure what I was doing was right.

The one thing I did know was that eventually I wanted it to be more than just beauty and fashion. That was good fun, but it didn't feel like a career centred on that had as much depth to it as I wanted.

In June 2012, it was decided I was now recovered enough that I was no longer benefiting from counselling so I was discharged. I felt like I had turned a corner, and felt confident and really pleased with myself for having worked through it all.

I made a decision. If I was going to continue with YouTube, and carry on amassing followers who repeatedly said they liked my honesty, then I really did have to be completely honest with them. So I sat down in front of my computer one day and, more nervous than I had been about any previous video, I spoke from my heart, trying to give my viewers as honest an account as I could of my recent activities and emotions. My mum and my sister were really worried about me putting myself out there like that, and weren't sure I would cope with negative feedback and any horrible opinions people would have about it, but I wanted my followers to get a glimpse of the real me behind the scenes. Actually more than a glimpse, a real clear view!

The resulting video was called 'The Pressure to be Perfect'. And wow, the response to that was incredible. It became my most watched video ever at the time (as I write this it is at 132,000 views), and I got a sudden influx of subscribers and social media followers. It seemed that people liked seeing more of what I was about, and the vulnerability that inevitably came with my honesty. In a world where every other YouTuber was doing their utmost best to present a picture of their life as more perfect than perfect, it seemed the honesty of this video touched a nerve. I wasn't showing off my latest cute dress, while clutching a miniature dog, in my fluffy pink girly room. I was opening myself up to let everyone see the damaged side of me.

The phrase 'role model' kept cropping up in the comments to my video and I was being sent private messages calling me that, and for the first time, I actually felt like I deserved the title. The way I saw it was if people thought I was a role model when I was being the real me and were inspired by me, then I was really proud and happy to be called that.

But the moment that stood out in my head more than anything was receiving a letter from a mum in Australia, who told me I had saved her daughter's life. She said she was in an eating disorder clinic, and underweight and unwell, but that she had loved watching my video, and it had given her the courage to carry on fighting to get better.

Some of the Letters I Received after 'The Pressure to be Perfect'

'I thought you were brilliant before your "The Pressure to be Perfect: My Story" video, but after watching that, I realised just how amazing you are. You are so wholly honest with your viewers about what you've been through and I really appreciate it – as do the rest of your viewers, I'm sure. My best friend committed suicide last May and I suffered for months with a bout of clinical depression. I self harmed for lack of any other outlet for what I was feeling and ended up planning my own suicide. I wish I'd found your channel earlier – maybe I wouldn't have even got to that stage. I can honestly say that you've saved my life. When I found your videos in my darkest days, I finally realised that it's true what all the doctors and therapists had been hollowly saying to me – I was not alone. Getting over depression was very much a DIY process for me – there was only so much that therapy and medication could do. I needed to relate to someone who I felt could really understand and I found that in you. I am so much more confident in myself, my abilities, my beliefs, my body. I no longer push myself. I've even started my own beauty blog, you being the biggest inspiration behind it! I've fully recovered from any disordered behaviours for 3 months, and off medication for 1 month. The truth, simply put, is this – I was swaying on the edge of a very high cliff and before I took that final step, you pulled me back and slapped some sense into me. Thank you, thank you, thank you.'

'Last November, my little sister died to leukaemia and ever since then I have been cutting. [...] Recently, I have been 1 month and 2 weeks clean and last night I felt the urge to cut again as I had a really shitty day. So I decided to go on your channel (my happy place) and watch your videos and something came over me and I felt fine again. The way you make us laugh and help us understand is enough to save someone (trust me). You have shown me not to care what anyone thinks and that I can dress how I like and be adventurous and still be confident!'

***

'Dear Gracie,

Going through hardship alone for so many years was not easy but coming across your videos and having someone I can relate to helped me more than I will ever know. I just wanted to let you know that there might be days when you don't think your videos and the things you talk about so passionately are pointless but I promise you they're not. Thank you for being there when nobody else was.'

***

'Dear Gracie,

I can't explain enough how grateful I am of you. Without your videos I'm not sure I would have got the help I needed. Your videos gave me the confidence that I needed to speak to people about my problems and because of this I was able to get the help that I needed. I used to watch your videos every morning before school to calm me and give me the push that I need because going out of my home fills me with anxiety and your videos minimised some of the anxiety. I have now left therapy but still have my down days in which I turn to your videos to help me get through them. Even though you have problems of your own you have still managed to help so many other people with theirs which is just incredible.'

That is when I realised this was my thing, what I was passionate about, what gave me the most happiness, and I knew I had to take it further. I thought about the fact that it would be nice to take everything I was doing in the care home with the kids into the wider world. So that rather than helping four kids at a time, I could potentially reach hundreds, thousands, even millions! I like to think big and I believe it is great to challenge yourself and not set boundaries for your dreams. 'Gracie,' I told myself, 'we are going to take mental health to a global stage, no matter what this takes …'

Chapter 8
NO TOPIC IS TABOO

'Be you, bravely.'

The first time I had sex was in a field on a cold day, while dodging dog walkers, with the noise of the motorway providing the 'romantic music'. How's that for a first time?!

Actually, from the stories I've heard from other mates and people over the years, as first times go it was not as bad as it sounds. At least the guy was my long-term boyfriend, he treated me very well, and we cared a lot about each other.

He was called Alex and we had met when I was in Year Ten. He was at my school but in the year below me, so I didn't know him, although he was very popular with the girls, as I was to find out. He was also at my stage school, but again we hadn't mixed there. It was only on the set of *Harry Potter* that we started hanging out, as he was working on the film as an extra like me.

We didn't tell people we were dating in the beginning because of the year gap. I know that is so irrelevant as you get older, but at school it was weird being with a guy in the year below! One day, not knowing we were together, a friend of his said to him:

'Grace would be the hottest girl in school if she just lost some weight.' When I found out I didn't know whether to feel happy or sad, as it was like a backhanded compliment. I had the potential to be hot, but my weight, as ever, was getting in the way. But actually Alex was always supportive in that respect, and never made me feel bad about my weight or insecurities. Looking back he was a really kind and mature kid for his age.

It was a healthy relationship, and we didn't really row. There wasn't the obsession and crazy love that there had been with my first boyfriend Aaron, but we had a lot of fun together and Alex was very respectful to me. We had kind of spoken about having sex, and I was keen to finally lose my virginity as it felt like EVERYONE else had already had sex (they hadn't).

Alex felt like the right person for me to have my first time with; I was old enough and mature enough to have made a grown-up decision that the time was right for me, and it was a safe and loving relationship. But when the field visit happened it was spontaneous, and not exactly full of the romance and passion I had imagined I would experience during my first time.

We had gone to the cinema, and then were wandering in a nearby field afterwards, when things got heated and before I knew it we were having sex. While it wasn't exactly candles and rose petals, it certainly gave us something to laugh about, and ever since then I have felt that fun, laughter and cheekiness is an important part of good sex.

Perhaps because we were in a proper relationship and he treated me well, it really felt like we were in it together. It is so important for your first time that you are with someone you trust, that you are both consenting, and it is a safe environment (OK, I realise I failed on the last). In fact they should be crucial every time you have sex.

I remember my first time didn't hurt which worried me, so I went home and told my mum. She said it was probably because I was a dancer, my hymen would have broken before without me noticing. We discussed things like that, me and Mum, we had a very open relationship in discussing sex, which has probably helped me to be as open about it as I am today.

Touch of my Hand

While Alex was my first when it came to sex, I had been experimenting with my body long before that, by myself. Masturbation. Oh yes, guys, I just said it, *that* word. How does it make you feel? Embarrassed? Happy? Ashamed? Excited? Dirty?

These days I'll happily chat about it and not bat an eyelid, but wow, I remember how much of a no-go it was at school, a shameful word that you just didn't say, no matter what. One time someone did mention it, everyone was like, 'Oh my God, that is disgusting!' Whereas my response was different. 'Oh my God, totally!' I agreed, nodding my head like mad. Then I laughed to myself, because the reality was I was thinking, 'I did that last night, before I went to sleep.'

I can't even remember when I first masturbated, but I know by the time I was about thirteen I was masturbating pretty much every night. I remember this really weird old American sex show called *Sexcetera* was on about 10.30 p.m., and I'd sneakily put it on in my bedroom when I was supposed to be asleep. They would talk about fetishes and I learnt all about bodies and sex from it. That show formed an embarrassingly big part of my sex education, if I'm honest. Then I would masturbate before I went to sleep, and I remember thinking, 'This is just the greatest thing ever.' I could sleep easier, and wake up feeling fresher, ready to take on the world.

But the topic was so totally and utterly taboo amongst my female friends. Boys, on the other hand, would proudly talk about their experiences all the time – at so many opportunities, in fact, that it got boring. 'I had a wank last night' they would announce loudly, looking for a reaction. Did you, well done you.

But for girls, uh-uh, off the radar, no-go. Admitting to such a thing would be like social suicide. Even the number of female singers that have included it in their songs didn't help – shout out to Janet Jackson, Pink, Britney Spears, my girl Christina Aguilera and all the rest.

It was only as I have got older and more sexually liberated and able to talk about sex in general that I have felt able to discuss masturbation. Once I had broken down that barrier, it was suddenly like, 'Oh, this is perfectly OK to talk about, why don't more people do so?' In fact why don't teenagers stop pretending, and start discussing the reality of it? The perception is that for females it must be a dirty, weird thing to do because it is such a taboo topic, but it is not, it is perfectly normal. I repeat, IT IS PERFECTLY NORMAL! So we need to make a conscious effort to talk about it and get rid of the old-fashioned stigma around it.

Let's face it, if you look at it from a biological point of view, women have a clitoris, and what is its function? Absolutely nothing beyond pleasure. It does nothing. It has literally no role in life beyond to be touched and make a woman feel amazing. So what is so wrong with doing what nature intended?

All sorts of crazy myths have sprung up over time, relating it to infertility, blindness, insanity . . . but the reality is that studies have actually shown that masturbating can make you healthier, happier, reduce stress, and increase the quality of your skin. If that was anything else in life that made all those things happen, you would be doing it all the time and talking about it until the cows came home. So shake off your embarrassment and spread the word!

Masturbating

- Releases dopamine, which activates pleasure in the brain and reduces stress levels.

- Releases endorphins and oxytocin that decrease your pain perception and can reduce period pains.

- Reduces stress hormones in the body, which in turn lowers inflammation. This has benefits for your skin – as well as the short-term post-orgasm glow, over time it can help reduce wrinkles and even reduce acne.

- Helps prevent cervical infections and relieves urinary tract infections, as the increased fluid flushes out bacteria.

- Helps fight insomnia, thanks to the fact it helps release hormones and tension.

After I broke up with Alex – no explosive ending, it just kind of fizzled out – I dated a couple of other guys, and also began to experiment with girls. Growing up, I always knew I liked girls. I got my first glimpse of lesbian porn when I was thirteen as the boys in school had worked out how to find it on the internet and get clips on their phones. I enjoyed it, and would spend hours poring over pictures of women's bodies in newspapers and magazines. But I was confused. I couldn't work out if I actually fancied them, or if I was just fascinated by them. While I was busy hating my own body, these girls had perfect curves and were toned in all the right places, so I wasn't sure if I was pining after their bodies as I wanted to *be* that girl, or I wanted to *be with* that girl.

The world of performing arts is stereotypically pretty sexually open-minded and liberated, and that was certainly true of my stage school. People were openly gay, lesbian, straight, or experimenting, and it was all considered completely normal. No one batted an eyelid, whatever you were, and my friendship circle was a mix of all sexualities.

One night when I was sixteen, a female friend and I got a bit drunk on WKD, and began kissing. Things escalated rapidly and we ended up fooling around. Thanks to the alcohol I can't remember who initiated it, or too much detail, although I know I came away from it having enjoyed the experience. It was like, 'This is great, when can I try that again?!'

After that I began having occasional flings with girls, mainly friends, who were also keen to try out new things. All my stage school friends were experimenting together and not caring who thought what, because there wasn't that judgement. I remember being half asleep in a room after a party once, and realising two of the guys in the same room were getting pretty heavy with each other. I just rolled over, closed my eyes, let them get on with it and went back to sleep.

We were all finding out who we were, and although I don't remember ever analysing what we were doing, thinking or feeling, it wasn't really a big thing to me and didn't hinder me being who I am. It boiled down to sexual pleasure, and I didn't overthink it. It was a chance to see what we wanted to do, and just felt like very normal, liberated teenage behaviour.

I like the fact that despite all the shit I was going through in my teen years, and the lack of confidence I had in so many areas of my life, I still did this. It is a nice feeling to look at my childhood self and think, 'You must have had some sort of self-belief to do all that, and more importantly, to enjoy it!'

My Year of Sexual Liberation

When I was in my early twenties I lost a lot of weight as had been suggested to me by the counsellor, and on the surface at least, it gave me much more confidence than I had felt in a long time – if ever. I also felt sexier and very aware of the looks I was beginning to get from others, and the flirtatious comments. At the same time my awareness was growing of just how toxic my relationship was with Demi, and that neither of us were making each other happy. We were together on and off for five years, always breaking up but always boomeranging back to each other. This time I knew we needed to split up, and for good. I think he assumed we were on yet another of our breaks, but I knew this was it. I knew it was time for us both to move on, so when he wanted us to get back together, I was adamant we were over.

Instead I booked a holiday to Turkey with a friend, and had a great time just drinking, partying, and revelling in my new appearance and confidence. I came back looking really brown, healthy and happy. Combine that with the confidence boost I was getting in my job at the care home, and my new YouTube hobby, and I finally felt that life was going somewhere.

But what to do about boys? I decided I was going to go on lots of dates but not get tied down to anyone. I didn't want relationship worries, but I wanted to have fun and learn more about myself, my own body, and sex in general. I had spent so long hating myself for my weight and appearance, and then for the sexual assault, that I decided it was time to put that behind me and think about me and what I wanted, for once.

I signed up to loads of dating sites – Plenty of Fish was my favourite – and just generally made sure to be open-minded, while staying safe, and to trust my instincts. Soon I was going on dates every week, and not judging myself on how I behaved, but just going with the flow of whatever felt right in each situation. Don't get me wrong, I wasn't jumping into bed with all these guys; a lot of the time I was just there for the banter and flirtation, to have fun and enjoy the compliments. But if anything more happened, then that was fine too.

It was a year of promiscuity that was completely different to what I had gone through when I was punishing myself after the assault. That was a hellish period of my life with guys and was all about giving them what I thought they wanted, while I had no real say over my body. This time it was the reverse. I really put my own needs, feelings and enjoyment first, and explored my own body, working out what I liked. I also learnt about other people's bodies and what turned them on, but after so long of coming second, I was determined that my pleasure was going to come first. Oh yeah.

The whole year was a great experience and I was becoming comfortable with being naked, and who I was, and I was learning not to be ashamed about anything. Generally I was loving life and learning that it was fun to be a woman, and to be me.

During this time, I was still having other relationships with girls too, but I never wanted anything more than sex from it. I never wanted a fling to turn into a relationship. I never saw any of the girls as a long-term partner the way I did with boys.

I had some serious crushes on famous women, though. Step forward Christina Aguilera, Adrienne Bailon, and the Pussycat Dolls – yup, every single member of the group!

I rarely set out to instigate sex. I wouldn't be sitting at a party, desperate to be with a particular girl. But sometimes I would be out socialising, feel in the mood, be chatting to a friend who seemed equally in the same space, and we would end up having fun together, however far that meant it went.

I didn't talk to my family about it, or my school friends really, who were all straight and would have turned it into something it wasn't. As far as I was concerned it was my personal journey of sexual exploration and not theirs, so really it was none of their business.

I haven't had sex with a girl for quite a while now. The fact I haven't since is not because I don't want to, but because I have been in a long-term relationship for the last two and a half years, and it wouldn't be right.

I have thought a lot about it since and whether I am straight or bisexual, and to be honest I am a bit conflicted over it. Sometimes

I think I am bisexual as come on, let's face it, girls are much sexier beings than men, lol! They are more soft and sensual, and ooze a lot more sex appeal.

But I like receiving more than doing when I am having sex with a girl, and I am not sure what that means. Am I just selfish when it comes to pleasure? Maybe the brutal truth for me is man or woman – who cares? As long as you can satisfy me, babes, I'm happy!

I have kind of come to the conclusion that I would rather not label myself and my sexuality, and sometimes people have reacted to that by asking: 'Why, are you ashamed of what you are?' but it is not that at all. It is just not that big a deal for me. Maybe I am bisexual, and that is fine. Maybe, as it has been a few years since I was with a girl, it was a phase, and that is OK as well.

I see it that you be you, I'll be me, and it's as simple as that. Maybe we don't need labels. Maybe we should just let people be who they are, and that should be enough.

One thing I learnt to really believe in during that year is the fact that yes, my orgasm is as important as his. This whole idea that sex is still primarily for the man's pleasure still ridiculously prevails in so many circles, but I ain't having it!

Not to blame porn for everything – as there are good things about it – but I do think it is partly at fault. Think of any porn scenes you have seen – nine times out of ten the guy finishes and that is it, game over. Absolutely fucking not, pull yourself together and tend to the girl's needs too, please! There are two of you tango-ing, OK? So get back to it and make sure she finishes this as happy as you.

Honestly, the idea that the pleasure is all for men really annoys me. It is another one of those society-created double standards that cause women to feel a sense of shame if they want an orgasm. It originates from this ancient idea perpetuated when men were in charge and trying to keep control of their women. So they decided that women should only want to partake in sex to have a baby, but should never want to have sex for pleasure.

It is not just old-fashioned, it is also sexist, plain ignorant, and actually quite sad. Are you feeling my anger vibes?! What do men think the clitoris was invented for if it was not for pleasure? I have heard it first-hand from plenty of boys that actually they enjoy sex a lot more if they know the girl is happy too, really happy, not in a fake porn kind of a way. It is like some people watch porn, see the girl screaming her head off pretending she is having a great time, so a teenage boy just thinks, 'Right, I've just got to stick my dick in her, pump really hard, and she will love it.' No, babes, no! That is not how it works. Ugh.

I will never forget one specific time during my year of liberation, when I had become surer of myself and my body, and was confident that I wasn't just there to provide pleasure for a man, but it was a two-way street. I had a good friend who I had known since I was sixteen, who was successful and well-known. I had always fancied him and over the years it became obvious that the sexual chemistry went both ways. So in this year of confidence and experimentation, it just so happened that we had the conversation about how we did both fancy each other, and we both knew that inevitably at some point we would end up having sex.

So I decided to move it along a bit, and invited him over one evening. He arrived and instantly kissed me, but it felt really awkward. It didn't bode well, but I told myself to stick with it and we would see. Maybe we just needed to get past the weirdness of the fact we were friends. Within minutes he was pulling my clothes off, no foreplay or anything, then suddenly we were having sex. I laid there, kind of surprised, thinking I'm not really into this. He is not kissing me or paying any attention to me. I may as well be a corpse lying here while he gets off on it. You don't just kiss someone then the next minute think you can have your dick in them without paying any attention to them at all. I need sex to be funny, cheeky and pleasurable. There needs to be foreplay and affection, attention and emotion.

Now a couple of years before that, I would have just lain there and put up with it. Assumed as a girl that as long as he was happy and enjoying it, that was what really mattered. Uh-uh, no way babes, not by this stage.

'Get out,' I said, pulling back.

'What?'

'You are obviously having a great time, but I'm not into it. It is all about you, and I could be anyone right now, so we are just going to stop.'

He couldn't believe it. Because of his job he was used to living like a king, girls falling at his feet, and him getting whatever he wanted from them, so because I wasn't behaving like that he was shocked. I told him that he had made me feel like a piece of meat and that just lying there to let him finish was not cool. It was a case of stop! Penis exit!

He was furious and pulled his clothes on and stormed out.

There was no sitting and having an adult conversation about what went wrong. That was the end of that. We still have the odd bit of contact, but I don't think his ego liked what happened that day. I'd like to think he might have learnt something from it, and treated the next girl with a bit more respect in the bedroom, but sadly, I am not convinced. For men like that it is even harder than it is for ordinary guys to see real life and the role of women for what it is.

I hope women too are learning to think more like that and show their boyfriends and husbands the way they should be treated, and what they want in bed. The idea of having sex just because it fulfils your partner's needs is a very sad way to be and means a lot of people are missing out on what could be amazing sexual experiences – because when it is done right, sex is frigging amazing!

Things I Wish I Had Known Before I Had Sex

- It is nothing like the movies. There is a lot of fumbling, weird noises, mistakes . . . but embrace them as part of it.

- You will sweat, look like a mess, and end up with blotchy skin.

- It's not unusual to find you can't orgasm through penetrative sex. The clit is your best friend.

- It doesn't always hurt. Society tries to deter females from having sex by saying it will be painful or uncomfortable, but that is not always true. Like I said, losing my virginity was actually painless.

- Foreplay is often the best part (it is for me anyway). The build up to sex is sometimes better than the act itself.

- It won't always last long.

- Have a pee afterwards, to help prevent cystitis.

I was on the pill throughout this time – I had gone on it at seventeen years old – so there has pretty much never been any chance of me getting pregnant. But I hold my hands up; in the past I haven't always been careful with condoms, even with a new partner. I was always careful after any slip-ups though to go to the clinic and get checked out. Back when I was a teenager that was more like a day trip out with your friends. Cinema? Shops? Nah, let's go and get swabs taken and piss in a pot . . .

The only time I did catch an STD was with an ex, as it turned out he was cheating on me when we first got together. But I dealt with it quickly, and it actually made my self-care sexually become extremely good. I would never slip up like that again. Full-on protection from the start now, unless we have both made the decision, and gone to get tested together, and then are in a committed relationship just with each other. Your sexual care is not a joke and the sooner you get with it, the better. I cannot emphasise how important protection is in terms of avoiding STDs and unwanted pregnancies.

The contraceptive pill is a funny thing for me, though. I have tried a few over the years, changing for various reasons, and it would be a massive lie to say that it didn't give me lots more sexual freedom and peace of mind in terms of not becoming pregnant.

But recently I have taken myself off it. As a teenager I had just taken it without question. Everyone else took it so of course it was fine, why wouldn't I? But now I am older I have begun reading up on it more, and I am shocked at the articles I have been reading linking mental health and depression with the pill. I shouldn't be surprised really. We are putting hormones into our bodies that wouldn't naturally be there. Besides it was only invented in the 1960s, so it hasn't been around long enough for us to understand all the long-term effects. So I am no expert – and please everyone do your own reading up on it before making any decisions – but I decided that I wasn't OK with it. Now I am just waiting for there to be a decent pill for men to take, so they can deal with the responsibility and all the crap put in to their bodies for a bit, instead!

Thrush

Ahh, the joy of thrush. Another one of those things no one else seems to talk about, so I feel the need to talk to you gorgeous people on the topic.

Let's get a few things clear about thrush from the off:

1. It is not a sexually transmitted disease.

2. It is not something you get because you are 'dirty'.

3. Around 75 per cent of women will suffer with it at some point in life, so if you haven't already had it, you should wise up on it, as chances are you will need to know!

When I was twelve years old I was filming for a TV show called *Star*, an ITV series that starred Nicholas Hoult and Hannah Tointon. I was on set, but I didn't feel right. I could feel my vagina kind of pulsating, as though there was an eel wriggling around in my pants making me feel really uncomfortable. Yeah, I know that is weird, but it is the best description I can think of!

It turned out I had a water infection and thrush. I had no idea what it was at the time or what was causing it, but I had to learn quickly, as from then on, it got worse and worse and has been the bane of my life ever since.

By the time I was eighteen, I was suffering every month from thrush – or candidiasis, if you want to get medical. And not just an uncomfortable itch like some people get, but a horrific, burning pain, combined with a weird discharge.

Thrush is basically a yeast infection caused by a change in your PH balance. It is common in pregnant women and babies, but can happen at any point in life with all sorts of factors contributing, from the contraceptive pill, to stress, to antibiotics.

Doctors were never able to specifically say what was causing it for me, but being monthly it might have been linked to my period in some way, or I could have just been prone to it. Interestingly, though, some recent research is even looking at the idea that it might be linked with trauma, and given the amount of that I have gone through, I'm clearly going to be living with thrush for the rest of my fucking life, haha.

Like so many other topics I don't really understand why thrush is taboo. The idea that it is dirty or linked to an STD is just ignorant, and behaving like it is something to be ashamed of just adds to the shit that the sufferer is going through. But of course as a teenager I wasn't going to be the person to try and break that perception, so I kept quiet, and went through it on my own. There is nothing worse than doing a dance show or a rehearsal, and sweating like mad in your leotard, while your vagina is throbbing with pain.

Tiny newborn
me with mum.

Developing my
love of crisps at
an early age!

Learning to punch!
I was such a cute
toddler, if I do say
so myself.

On a family trip to Bournemouth when I was 11-years-old. I wouldn't take my shorts off because I thought my legs were too fat.

At a school fete. I loved face paints and the Spice Girls at the time, hence the pose!

The letter I wrote as a 9-year-old, already conscious of my weight.

Dear Mum

How are you? I'm o
I hope by the Summe
I will have lost some
weight thankes for the
christmas Presents I
really liked them. I'm gb
I'mdoing Jhoesph

LoVe

From.

XGrace xxxs

Hanging out with my friend Lauren from Jackie Palmer's.

On a day out at Thorpe Park with Beno, Roz and Marvyn, friends from stage school.

Trying life as a blonde, with my sister on my 24th birthday. You can see I am thinner as I was restricting.

With my lovely sister Charlotte, when I was 19. Everyone always says we look alike.

#STYLE
HAS
NO
SIZE.

EVANS

Above: At a party for Evans, with Callie and Louise.

Below: Me and Simon always have a laugh together. Messing around on Instagram and at New Year's Eve this year.

Opposite: Relaxing with Danie at her family home in Devon.

This was a body positive post on Instagram about unflattering angles and the fact you never see images of girls showing their rolls.

Relaxing around the pool with my body positive crew, Olivia, Danie and Callie.

With Stormzy
and the other
girls on set
to record the
video for *Big
for Your Boots*.

Hanging out
with Callie.

Me and Erica,
a close friend
from the States.

On a recent trip
to the US to see
my gorgeous
girlies out there.

Happy, just being me.

Canesten cream became my best friend, and then I discovered apple cider vinegar. This is a great home remedy, poured in your bath. Yes, you might come out smelling a bit like a chip shop, but hey, it does the trick!

I obviously wasn't sexually active when I first suffered from it, but over time I had to broach the subject with several boyfriends and explain to them what it was. They had hardly ever heard of it, so I ended up educating them, and fair play to them, they all took it well.

So yeah, chances are you will have it at some point, but at least you will know what to do now. Just make sure you take care of your delicate little petal!

Sex – The Facts

I have been thinking a lot lately about sex and the expectations there are on girls in terms of what you should do, when you should do it, what is for one-night stands, what you should save for boyfriends etc, as it seems to me that as time goes on you are expected to be sexually savvy from a young age, and to perform all sorts of acts.

So for me, from about fourteen years old the expectation in school was that if you had a boyfriend, you were going to be sexually active. At that time, that was the norm, so actually I was a bit on the late side. But no one actually talked about the sex they were having or what they were doing, other than in really vague terms. It was just a case of saying you had had sex. Or that you had been fingered. 'Oh yeah, he fingered me last night' was the most sexual thing I said when I was in my mid-teens.

Fast forward to 2017, and they are waaaaay past all that, despite the fact that it remains illegal in the UK for anyone to have sex with a person who is under the age of sixteen. Now, young people are still becoming sexually active around the same age, but there is no build-up to anything. It is like you snog a boy, and half an hour later he is expecting anal sex, doggy-style over the kitchen counter, or for the girl to be performing all kinds of crazy shit.

And the reason it has gone this in-depth? Porn. Boys have so much access to it these days and are watching so much of it, that they are getting completely warped expectations. They follow porn stars on Instagram and think all naked girls will look like that, and believe that the things these girls are doing should be the kind of things their fourteen-year-old girlfriend is also prepared to do.

Seriously, the pressure on a poor fourteen-year-old girl today is insane. She is expected to have perky tits, a big bum, slim thighs, a flat stomach, thin arms and a neatly tucked, waxed vagina and arsehole. She should be street smart, book smart, and able to perform just about any sexual trick under the sun. Who the fuck is like that? No one, and it wouldn't even be right if they were!

I would hear from the kids in the children's home all the time what they were being asked to do, and I hear it from my followers on YouTube. Someone needs to get a grip on it all, but I am not sure who or how. I can't see it swinging back the way parts of America have done with their chastity rings etc., but honestly, it scares me to imagine what will be expected of kids in as little as ten years' time . . . Oh my God, if I have a daughter I am going to be stressed out of my mind!

One thing I learnt while writing this book was about the origin of the word blowjob. There are loads of theories as to where the name comes from, but the one that stuck in my head was that in the 1930s when guys were working on the ships and stopped for some time on land, they would hunt out local prostitutes and hire them. But if they wanted fellatio, this was such a rare and exotic thing to happen that it cost them a lot of money. The prostitutes were canny enough to know exactly how much money the sailors were paid, and would ask for that amount. So they basically had to 'blow' all their cash on that one 'job' by the prostitute.

Who knows if that is the genuine origin, but it is fascinating to think that less than a hundred years ago, a blowjob was considered something so alien and perverted that only a prostitute would do it, and for a lot of cash. Doesn't half prove my point about how sexual expectations have changed so rapidly over time . . .

Is Porn a Good or a Bad Thing?

Sometimes it seems like we are all feeling our way in the dark when it comes to sex – literally and metaphorically!

It is such a minefield and can leave a lot of people feeling confused as they learn about it. It is one of the reasons I try and talk so openly about it on my channel and do all I can to stop it being a taboo subject.

One of the areas of sex that comes up time and again is porn. I am fine with it in theory and have watched plenty of it myself, but there are so many negative aspects to it as well. Things that are worth considering:

Reasons to watch it:

- Parents and schools generally try to educate kids on sex but they don't always do a great job, so watching porn can go some way to giving people a basic grounding.

- If there is an area of sex you want to know about but are too afraid to ask others, you can look into it alone in private.

- For people who have questions about their own sexuality, watching different types of porn can sometimes help them work it out.

- Porn includes all kinds of sex so it can give you fresh ideas, make a person feel more liberated, and spice up your sex life.

Reasons to avoid it:

- Let's face it, no one actually has sex the way they do in porn films! I certainly don't anyhow . . . So it can lead to people having unrealistic expectations in the bedroom.

- There is still a real focus on the man's pleasure in porn, so teenage boys who watch lots of it can get the idea that it is all about them, and become very focused on what they want to get out of sex, rather than also considering what their girlfriend might enjoy.

- There is hardly anything in porn that connects love and sex, so the impression is that sex is all about one-night stands, and never within loving relationships. If a person gets addicted to porn it can prevent them from forming real-life relationships.

- A viewer can easily be drawn into darker areas of porn thinking it is ok as it is just onscreen, but this can normalise areas such as underage sex or rape.

- Porn stars' bodies are very much of one type, and again can give people false expectations of the other sex, as well as giving people added insecurities about their own bodies. It can make people conscious of flaws in body parts they may never have considered before.

- Porn is too easily accessible on the internet now, so children that are too young to be exposed to certain aspects of sex are able to find it. It needs more policing from parents, schools and social media.

I feel like vaginas need a bit of a shout out in this section too because, well, a) they are super special, but b) I am worried the way this whole designer vagina thing is kicking in. It is wrong!

I never thought too much about what mine looked like when I was a kid, apart from when it started to sprout hair – honestly, that was another thing that happened early; I was like a full-blown woman by the time I was ten. I remember seeing these hairs start to appear, and thinking, 'I'm not OK with this, what the hell are you, big bush growing down below?!' But beyond the usual 'stick a mirror on the floor and inspect it' at some point, I just assumed my vagina looked like everyone else's.

It was only when I first watched porn that I realised all the different types there are, or that things like their shape, or the size of the lips, could vary so much. I also didn't know that people got rid of all their hair either. Whenever it was discussed at school it was considered pretty risqué to get a landing strip, but no one would ever talk about getting it all taken off. A fully waxed or shaven one would have been like, oh my God.

But all these porn stars are completely hairless, and also have bleached arseholes. I mean, come on . . . The increase in access to porn has now led to lads today having bizarre expectations of vaginas. They assume they are meant to be hairless, and find it weird when they see hair. There is now a perception of exactly what size everything should be, and people going in for labia reductions.

Yes, look after your fanny and groom it however you like, but don't just conform to yet another male-imposed ideal – I promise you, whatever you have down there is just perfect and any boy with half a brain will love it just the way it is!

My year of liberation came to an end when I started dating my next serious boyfriend, Simon. I knew I liked him and wanted to commit to him, so that was the end of all other sexual encounters – male and female! Instead I focused on building up a great sex life with Simon. Fun though my 'try anything' year was, sex within a long-term, trusting relationship really is the best kind.

Chapter 9
HOW LOSING WEIGHT MADE ME FAT

'When you look in the mirror and don't like what you
see, society needs to change, not you.'

Up until a couple of years ago I had spent my whole life thinking about what I was eating. Every single meal, every single day, for as long as I could remember.

If I restricted what I was eating, counted calories and ate something that was deemed healthy, I would feel good about myself. I'd congratulate myself: 'I've got through this day without eating fattening food, yay me!' and it was a massive thing on a personal level.

But if I ate something unhealthy, I'd be plagued with an overwhelming sense of guilt, combined with shame and embarrassment and I'd lie in bed that night unable to sleep, scared that I was going to put on weight. 'Have you no willpower, Grace?

When you get fatter, it will be no one's fault but yours! Gotta do better tomorrow.'

I assumed this was a normal thought process, and that it must be what went on in the minds of everyone else too. I figured everyone must calorie count, because for people to be thin they would have to restrict their intake and think about every single meal. How else would they be able to keep their enviable figures?

It wasn't the only assumption I made about weight either. I assumed that because all the successful people I saw on television and in the media were thin, I needed to be thin too. All my life I believed that if I lost weight, everything else would be fixed. Any issue with my family, friends, money, career, boys, would all work out if I could only just change and become 'one of the thin people' . . .

When I was twenty-one I began seeing a counsellor who, as I mentioned earlier, noticed from the off that I was unhappy with my weight. She very quickly decided that this was the root of my unhappiness and recommended that it would be beneficial to me to lose a few pounds. The implication was that my depression and unhappiness was caused because I was fat. That fitted perfectly with the way my mind already worked, so I readily accepted what she was saying.

I had ballooned to 18½ stone at the time, thanks to keeping up the eating habits I had developed while bulimic, but no longer making myself sick afterwards. The fact I moved so little and struggled to even get out of bed because of the depression had not helped either. I was the most unhappy I had ever been in my life, and that was reflecting itself in my body.

'Lose weight,' the counsellor told me. 'Go to Weight Watchers, get some weight off you, and that will help.'

So I did. I signed up to my local group and began eating healthily (or what I thought was healthy eating at the time), and reading all the self-help books I could get my hands on. I also started exercising. I signed up for Zumba classes, started swimming, and went to the gym four times a week. I would use those vibration plate machines, the ones that promise that if you exercise on them, it will jiggle all your fat away! Oh my God, how desperate must I have been at that time for a quick fix, that I could bear to stand there, wobbling all over the place in the name of weight loss!

I did actually enjoy exercising on some level, but it wasn't because I was trying to be fit and healthy, or that I was getting a thrill out of the athletic achievements. It was because I knew it would help me lose weight and look better. Each jiggle on those plates took me a step closer to that beautiful thin physique that I so wanted.

And of course, the weight started falling off me. Restricting food and constantly exercising will do that; there are no complicated science equations needed for that to happen.

But what spurred me on more than what I was seeing in the mirror or in my shrinking dress sizes were the compliments that began flowing from friends, family, even strangers. People were giving me that instant feelgood factor when they said to me: 'Wow, look at you! You look so good now, Grace!' 'Losing weight really suits you; you should have done that ages ago!'

I even stopped self-harming, as it was no longer the release of pain through cutting myself that made me feel good, but the opinions of others. The more they told me I looked good, the more I felt popular and validated as a person. The compliments were rapidly becoming my new addiction.

When my weight loss slowed up and I decided Weight Watchers was no longer doing its job, I switched to Slimming World, and religiously followed their menus and 'syn system'. It gave me a second burst of weight loss, and the pounds carried on dropping off, knocking 5 stone off in total and taking me down to 13½ stone.

So on the surface, I was much improved, and actually I did believe I was getting better. Get skinny, fix your problems! It seemed like it was coming true. Work was great, I had built up the confidence to split from a negative relationship and I was getting lots of male (and female) attention. I was literally going, 'Yeah, girl, your life is sorted, this is it!'

But underneath all the surface improvement, let's take a look at what had really happened . . .

1. First, the counsellor had confirmed my deep-rooted belief that being skinny was what would make me better. She zeroed in on weight as though that was the reason behind everything that was going wrong in my life and reiterated the idea that self-worth is based on what you look like. In retrospect she should clearly have focused on the mental issues linked to my weight, and got to the root cause of them. But instead the idea was reinforced that I should change my body for others as that is what would make me happy as a person.

2. Weight loss is obviously not always a bad thing, but it needs to be done in the right way, and I wasn't doing it in a healthy manner. I had become obsessed with it. There wasn't a moment when I wasn't trying to lose weight, and I always had a new goal, whether it was a smaller size of jeans or a compliment from a certain person.

3. As a result, my relationship with food, which hadn't been great at the best of times, had become completely disordered and out of control. Everything from my thoughts to my portion sizes had taken on a life of their own – but dangerously I thought I *was* in control, so was always restricting that bit more.

4. Despite everything, despite the fact I thought about food every second of every day and don't think I could have been doing any more to physically change myself, I still didn't like the way I looked. Yes, of course I loved what people were saying to me, but I didn't actually believe them. My mind had not changed along with my body, so I hated myself as much as I had before. Being skinny hadn't made one tiny bit of difference to how I really thought of myself.

So let's face it, this was never going to be sustainable, no matter how much I wanted it all to work, was it? It was a short-term solution, like putting a little sticking plaster over a bloody great wound. For two years I pushed on with it, dieting, exercising, believing if I could just be a bit thinner, I would be happy. I was in this constant cycle of always trying to lose weight, and if I did lose weight, of then trying to keep it off. It felt like I was forever fighting against this constant tide, and if I took my eye off my weight for even a second, I would drown. So each day it was a mental struggle to get to the gym and then to analyse everything I was eating that day and make sure there was no oil in it – I had a real issue with oil, and would obsess over it. Then I would worry about the most flattering angle I could take a photo from to make me look as thin as possible, or fret about how to deal with friends who wanted to go out to restaurants, where I didn't know what was in the food and had no control over the portion size.

I made sure I put on a show that I was happy, when really I was drained, and sick and tired of the constant worry of weight. I just wanted to be able to live a carefree life.

Then bam, twenty-four years old and it all blew up in my face. Suddenly I could no longer fight it. The pressures I was putting on myself had become too much and everything just crumbled around me. My obsession with eating the right food and relent-lessly exercising fell apart, and I woke up one day and just knew I couldn't keep up this constant battle to be thin any more. Now, instead of crying and starving myself if the Slimming World scales said I hadn't lost weight that week, I cried and ate. My food issues began playing out in a way I didn't think was possible – I began binge eating. And by that I mean I was eating and eating, any-thing I could get my hands on: take-outs (sweet and sour chicken was my fave), pizzas, Cadbury's chocolate . . . you name it. And I put on weight, and more weight and more weight, until I weighed the same as I had before I started dieting, and then some.

I carried on and on trying to battle it, but the thinner I tried to be, the bigger I got. The more I fought my weight, the worse it got, because my mind and my body were not matching up. What I now know is that changing weight does not change your mind-set. Being thin doesn't save you or make everything that is wrong in your life suddenly right. Being skinny doesn't suddenly give you magical confidence, self-belief, or change your world. But that is what I had failed to recognise. I thought if I was thin, my negative thoughts would be replaced by positive ones. But they weren't; my negative mind-set travelled right down the scales with me.

I always tell people: 'Love yourself at every size, whether that is as a twenty or an eight, it doesn't matter.' But I hadn't loved myself in either situation. I had hated myself when I was fat, and I hated myself just as much when I was thin. The mistake I made was thinking it would be otherwise.

Dieting Stats

- 65 per cent of dieters put the weight back on within three years.

- 40 per cent of extreme slimmers put more weight back on than before, and only 10 per cent actually manage to maintain it.

- People who regularly diet are five to twelve times more likely to binge eat.

I was still trying to fight this losing battle against my weight, when I came across a group of people who changed my life, and my way of thinking, forever – the body positive movement.

BODY POSITIVITY:
the acceptance of every body type, no matter what shape, size or colour. Inclusive of everyone, only body shaming is barred.

I was flicking aimlessly around Instagram one day when I came across a girl called Callie Thorpe. She caught my eye as she is a big girl and yet she was also really pretty, and happiness and confidence just kind of radiated off her pictures. OK, I thought, there must be a catch. So I started going through her photos, and the captions said things like 'living my best fat life!' and she was talking about loving herself and her body just the way it was. There was even a photo of her on holiday in a bikini, looking amazing, and she had a hot boyfriend who clearly loved her. This girl was living THE life.

Instagram algorithms meant other people like her were suggested to me, and soon I was trawling through all the photos of another girl called Danielle Vanier. She was also big, but had the most insane fashion sense, and looked incredible modelling all these bright patterns and statement outfits. Where was this girl shopping that she was able to find clothes like this?

As I searched I came across more and more of these larger girls who just gave off a totally inspirational vibe, such as Fuller Figure, Fuller Bust, and Body Positive Panda. They were fat but healthy, and loving life. It blew my mind! I learnt that they were part of what is known as the body positive movement. The key idea is the acceptance and celebration of every body type, particularly those that might not traditionally have been deemed beautiful. So whether a person is fat, has a disability, very dark skin, is transsexual, whatever . . . basically anything goes.

I spent hours trawling through all these pictures, staring in amazement at these girls' proudly posted photographs where they weren't posing to look slim or hide their flaws. These girls weren't trying to fit in, but were comfortable standing out. They would show their saggy boobs, stretchmarks and cellulite, imperfect skin tones, rolls, lumps and bumps – all problems I had myself, but somehow they were embracing them rather than hating and hiding them. It was like I was seeing a version of myself onscreen, but with the mind and attitude I wished I had. To me these people were true inspiration.

It was a whole new world to me, and I thought it was amazing. These people weren't trying to be thin or fighting to conform but were accepting of who they were. They were living proof that you could enjoy a healthy, happy life without having to be a size eight. People have different frames, bone structures, metabolisms and genes, so each person's natural size might not be super slim. Plus people go through different points in life where it is not always their priority to be in top shape – and they should not be made to feel bad for that. As a society we are failing to recognise this, but the body positivity movement was doing a damn good job of rectifying things.

It was exhilarating to be able to relate to other women who were bigger than what is 'acceptable' and to see them fighting back, and pulling up people on social media who were body shaming or being fatphobic. I wanted a piece of that! I knew it was revolutionary and discovering body positivity was going to change my life.

After that, I was constantly looking at these people's accounts, following them on other social media, and reading what they had to say. I began chatting with other people in the same position, and there was no extreme diet advice, or talk of plastic surgery, it was all just happy and fun. It was the first time I felt that I was part of a community where I was really accepted for who I was, and I began to feel good about myself.

As my confidence grew, I started to look at the people around me and think about whether they were adding anything positive to my life. I deleted any negative or diet-obsessed people I was linked with on social media, and stopped talking to real-life friends if they constantly made me feel as though I wasn't good enough. That wasn't ever an issue with this whole new bunch of people I was talking to; this community made me feel like I was *always* good enough, and for that they mean more to me than they will probably ever know. I met Callie and Danielle in real life and they were exactly like I imagined they would be from seeing them online, and became two of my best mates.

I began wearing clothes that I didn't previously think I could and I even got myself a bikini AND proudly took lots of photos of myself in it! Prior to that I had been obsessed with the fact that although I really wanted acrylic nails, they would make my hands look fatter. But my new friends encouraged me to go for it, and now I love my nails, and getting them done is one of life's small pleasures.

Basically the girls taught me about self-love and confidence. They inspired me to live life to the full, to do what I want to do, and to not let what I look like hinder me, and that is all I ever wanted really.

SELF-LOVE

Loving yourself whole-heartedly at every stage of your journey. It is about accepting yourself, looking after yourself and loving yourself as you would another. And telling everyone that says you aren't good enough to fuck off!

It was a slow process changing how my brain worked, and it didn't happen overnight, but bit by bit I began to learn how to really accept me for me. I was surrounded by so many people that loved themselves and showed me so much love that it was difficult to not start loving me too. It was like I actually got tired of hating myself, and realised the effort it took, how draining it was on me, and that I just wanted to be well and have a good life.

At the same time it was a massive help that I actually had a real-life example right in front of me. The fabulous Michelle, my boss at the kids' care home, was plus size, and totally owned it! She would call herself fat and just not care, and had such a positive outlook on life. It was the first time I had been around someone who understood and loved herself for who she was, whatever her weight. I remember thinking, 'Oh my God, this is weird. Actually, this is amazing, and exactly what I'm seeing online!'

The key to feeling brilliant about yourself is really learning to love your body type for what it is right now. OK, you can lose weight if you want to do so for yourself and it is coming from a kind place, but do not hate your body type for what it is today. There are other people in the world who look like you, so body positivity isn't just about you, it's also about considering other people's negative feelings about their bodies, and how you can provide a positive example to them. It is like feminism – in the way that is for all women everywhere, this is for all people and their bodies everywhere.

Everyone can – and should – talk about body positivity, and be body positive themselves. The movement has become so well-known across the world now that parts of it are even becoming a bit commercial, although they are still sanitised versions of it, i.e. the 'fat' model being used in an inclusive campaign will still have all her weight in the 'right' places – curvy hips, large boobs, but a flat stomach. So there is still a lot of work to be done, but it is a move in the right direction.

I was only sad I hadn't come across the movement earlier, but I am so glad for younger girls today that it is out there. I honestly think this movement, that I am really proud to now be a part of, is saving a lot of people's lives. So many young girls across the world are self-harming, have disordered eating, body image issues and are even committing suicide as a result of society's pressures. But these girls like Callie and Danielle – and now I like to think also me – are hopefully paving the way in changing attitudes.

Body Positive People Who Can Change Your Life!

If you want to get some body positive inspiration too, these are just a few of the accounts that I follow and that I promise will help get your mind into a more positive place!

Kenzie Brenna – @omgkenzieee

The Confidence Corner – @theconfidencecorner

Honor Curves – @honorcurves

F Your Beauty Standards – effyourbeautystandards

Simone Mariposa – simonemariposa

Olivia Campbell – @curvycampbell

Taylor Giavasis – @thenakediaries

Melissa Gibson – @yourstruelymelly

Tess Holliday – @tessholliday

Gabi Gregg – @gabifresh

Megan Jayne Crabbe – @bodyposipanda

Stefanie K – @_classycurves_

Kitty Underhill – @kittyunderhillx

Michelle Elman – mindsetforlifeltd

Tips for Being Body Confident at Every Size

- Take the negative connotations out of the word fat. It is a description, not an insult.

- Remember what is on the outside doesn't matter as much as what is on the inside.

- Imperfections are beautiful. Everything you are not, makes you everything you are.

- It is better to be a fat person than a bad person!

- Take away the power of others. So if an ex says you have gained weight, who cares, those people aren't important in your life. It is you and what you think that matters.

- Your body's main aim isn't to be aesthetically pleasing to others. Instead remember the real uses and look after it so it can perform those functions – legs are for walking, arms are to hug, breasts are to feed kids.

The more I came to understand that body confidence and self-love at all sizes is the way forward, the angrier I became with the diet industry, and diet culture as a whole.

Do you know dieting didn't even exist until the nineteenth century? Up until then the biggest worry was getting enough to eat, and if you did and you were fat, it didn't have the same negative connotations that it does today. It was the twentieth century before calorie counting became a thing, and even then it was so rare that the first book written about it actually had to instruct readers how to pronounce the word. So for thousands of years people have just got on with their lives, but in the last hundred we have become obsessed with weight and appearance. Oh, and that first book about calorie counting was aimed at women, there's a surprise . . .

Then in more recent years, with the emergence of the internet, diet culture has completely exploded. Everywhere you look there is some self-styled diet expert or nutritionist telling you what to do to get thin, have shiny hair, get glowing skin – and most of it is total bollocks! Seriously. I hate it more than anything. So much of it is just money-making crap that plays on people's insecurities.

Take Slimming World. I know loads of people swear by it and maybe it worked for them, but I really think you have to be honest with yourself and ask if it's actually getting to the root of your problem. The day I realised how ridiculous it was in my situation, I was looking at a list of my options and saw that an avocado was worth a lot more syns than I'd expected, for something that is good for you. But oh look, here is a chocolate bar, and that is only a few 'syns', so I may as well eat a few of them. And Diet

Coke? Well, that is zero points, so I can drink litres of that all day long! Does that sound like good advice to you? Argh, it makes me so angry, it's ridiculous.

Even the word 'syns' gets right on my nerves. It is obvious the link that is being made. Stop putting into people's heads that these foods are sins, just teach them to eat them in a balanced way! Yes, I understand that lots of people lose weight on the diet, myself included, but I don't believe it teaches you to eat well and intuitively, and look after your body and mind properly. I get so annoyed that I got sucked into it.

It is hardly like they are on their own, though. Everywhere you look there are people making money off this idea that we all have to look a certain way, weigh a certain amount, wear par-ticular-sized clothes if we want to be successful and valued and worthy. Some of this stuff may well help some people adjust to a healthy way of living but what they have in common is that they all play on women's insecurities, and I am not OK with it! All these fake food rules that you have to follow. How about we teach people to love themselves no matter what, and see if that doesn't make the world a better, happier place?

The Diet and Fitness Guidelines I *am* OK with . . .

To be clear here, I am obviously not saying that everyone should make a point of sitting on their sofas all day long, eating non-stop take-out, refusing to let any fruit or veg pass their lips. Having a healthy body is crucial on so many levels, such as if you are trying for a baby, want to tackle certain health issues, or would simply like to try and live as long a life as possible.

The key to it is remembering healthy and slim mean different things. Healthy might be a size eight or it might be a size eighteen, it is about understanding your own body and judging it on what feels healthy, not what you think it should look like.

So while I hate diets (have I made that clear yet?!) and don't like food rules, there are a few guidelines that everyone should try to follow purely for health and physical wellbeing. These are the ones that work for me:

- Don't think about what you *shouldn't* eat, or what you *should* eat – think about what your body is asking you to eat and learn to trust it.

- Get clued up on conscious eating – if you haven't come across this before, I explain it in Chapter 12.

- When reading any advice, make sure you sort the real dieticians/nutritionists/doctors from the fakes and *only* listen to them.

- Everyone needs to be active in some way, but it doesn't have to be about spending three hours a day in the gym. Find your own way to keep moving, whether that is walking the dog or hitting a club dance floor.

- Make sure you get a decent amount of sleep, and avoid stress. Both have a lot of impact on your physical wellbeing.

- Remember – everything you do should come from a kind place.

Stretchmarks

Oh my God. The dreaded bloody stretchmarks!

Growing up I always knew what stretchmarks were as my mum had developed quite a lot of them after her two pregnancies. But as far as I was concerned, that was the only excuse there was for having them – if they appeared at any other time, it just meant you were fat.

The first few I got appeared on my hips. I was horrified when I noticed them, even though they were very pale, but in a way I was actually able to live with them. Hips and bums were allowed to be curvy, because that is how boys like them, so if it meant I had a bit of weight on my hips, I could deal with it. It was my thighs and stomach that I was always obsessed with slimming down, followed by my arms and neck.

But then one day when I was fourteen years old, I woke up, started getting ready for school as normal, and froze as I looked over at myself in the mirror in my underwear. There, staring defiantly back at me, was a small thin line running down my stomach. I rubbed at it, hoping it was a crease mark from the way I had lain in bed. Nope. It was a fucking evil little stretchmark. Then and there I wanted to run down to the kitchen and get a knife to slice my stomach off. Why had this happened to me? I had lost lots of weight by now through restricting my eating and then throwing up, so surely it was wrong? Or did this mean I was getting fat again?

All day at school I felt sick. I kept my arms tight by my side so nothing rode up to expose my now grossly deformed belly. It was all I could think of; it took over my brain.

As I got off the bus with my friend Shannon at the end of the day, I couldn't wait to say 'goodbye' to her so I could get home and be alone. Then I sobbed and sobbed. I must have got instantly huge, a big whale who was eating too much, I decided. Otherwise why would it happen to me? I didn't realise it was a natural sign of growing, that there was nothing I could do as I grew and developed to stop my skin also having to stretch.

After that, more appeared. Over time I got them on my hips, stomach and arms. At first I did everything to fight them. Then as I got older, I started to see them on other people. I would be at the beach and see them all over the place on other women of all different ages and sizes, or a friend would undress, and I'd notice the odd one on them. The biggest revelation for me was later on when I got naked with a guy and saw he had them. I remember pausing and staring, while my brain shouted, 'Whoa, boys get stretchmarks too?!' It was a very liberating discovery, and made me less self-conscious of my own. I felt ridiculous to have worried over such a little thing. Does a shark worry that its fin mightn't be on perfect shiny form in the morning? Is a lion feeling sad because its mane isn't thick enough? No, as they are too busy eating, playing and actually living! Let's all be more lion and shark and get the fuck over ourselves!

Love your Boobs, and Your Nipples!

Just as I had really embraced and moved forward with the body positive movement, and learnt to love myself the way I am . . . I was offered a free boob job.

I have had a bit of a love/hate relationship with my boobs ever since they made themselves known when I was just ten years old – even at that age I was a B cup and needed a bra fitted. By my twenties I had obviously got a lot of pleasure out of them, but I was mad at them for being uneven sizes – my left is an E, and righty over there is an F – for being saggy, and for having inverted nipples.

I had long been dying to get my boobs operated on, so much so that when I was seventeen I had booked in for a consultation. I cancelled it at the last minute though as a) I got scared, and b) I realised I hadn't a hope in hell of affording the thousands of pounds it would cost, but the desire for it was still there, as freaking strong as anything.

My first issue with my boobs had been my inverted nipples. Before I knew what they were I would see my mum's boobs or those of girls in newspapers or magazines, and worry that my nipples were different. 'Why are mine flat? I don't I have the sticky-out bits,' I asked Mum. At ten she took me to the doctor, who told her: 'She has inverted nipples. Sometimes they pop out, sometimes they don't.'

All I remember taking away from it was the idea that 'God, I've got deformed tits.'

I was so concerned about it. I really thought I was the only person in the world to have them. When I got to thirteen I finally told a friend, and her reply was an absolute revelation. 'Grace, no way! I've got them too.' It was incredible, and made me feel that if I was odd, at least I wasn't being odd on my own!

At the same time they just kept getting bigger and bigger. I was fine with that, but then they started sagging too, and that I was not OK with, no siree. I'll have to have a boob job one day to make them perky, I decided. In the meantime I wore bras that were like armour, always did my bikini top up so tight that it held my boobs high up in place, and never dreamt of wearing backless or revealing tops that might give too much away about them.

I lived my whole life so self-conscious of them. I never wanted anyone to look at them or boyfriends to touch them. Whenever I had sex with someone for the first time the fact I had inverted nipples was the one thing I wanted to get out of the way so I would just kind of flag it up myself and laugh, as though it were fine, as though I had mocked myself before they could, when really it was so fucking awkward. But I was just so afraid that if they hadn't seen it before, and I don't suppose a lot of them had, if they touched my boob and tried to touch my nipple and there was nothing there for them to grab on to . . . well, that would be weird for both of us.

Throughout my teens I would often Google boob jobs. I hated the fact that they were different sizes. I was sure in my head that getting them fixed would go a long way to making me feel good about my own body.

Now at twenty-four, I finally had the chance to do what I had been wanting for years. A cosmetic surgery company were offering a free uplift in exchange for promotion on my channel, to get rid of the sagging, and an implant to improve the shape. My first reaction was to be really happy and book in straight away. I was going to look damn hot! But after a few days I started thinking. The idea was obviously that this would improve my boobs – but who was the judge of that? What right did anyone else have to decide for me how my boobs should look? Did this match up with everything else I was working on at the time? Was this the action of someone who was working towards body positivity? I thought about all the girls who had bravely posted pictures of their imperfect body parts in order to accept them, and to encourage others to embrace theirs. I had got to the point where I was a role model for lots of younger people, and I was telling everyone they needed to love themselves for who they are right now. If I was to get a boob job, that would send out the wrong message. Obviously it is up to anyone what they get in terms of surgery, and if it works for them, then that's cool. But in my opinion it would be wrong to preach self-love if I then went and fixed all the stuff I didn't like about myself.

No, getting a boob job seemed wrong.

The moment I said no was actually hugely liberating and empowering. It was when I realised I really do accept my boobs for what they are. Yes, they are saggy, I have massive areolas and inverted nipples, but they are soft, jiggly balls of fun, and I love them!

Instead of getting the surgery I went and talked about it on my channel and my blog and this time the media picked up on what I was saying and helped spread the word. This is one of the very reasons that I talk about these subjects, so people know they are not alone or isolated in feeling bad about their bodies and they can learn to love themselves too. Then I hope other people will carry it on and all talk to each other as well, and before you know it that is just how everyone will think, without it having to be an issue or a movement for change.

The irony is I have asked lots of boys about my inverted nippes and wonky boobs since, and really, they don't care. Most of them don't even notice, or if they do, it is not relevant to them. They are in the moment, and just happy that there are boobs there in front of them, whatever they look like! It is clear it was my own insecurities standing in the way of me accepting that all women's bodies are different, and all the better for being so. The obsession with perfection needs to end, and our differences should be celebrated.

Chapter 10
UNDER THE SPOTLIGHT

'The second greatest feeling on earth is having the courage to chase your dreams. The first is realising they are already coming true.'

I think it would be fair to say I have always been a bit of an underdog in the YouTube world. Apart from the fact that I look very different to a lot of my fellow influencers, my choice of taboo subjects definitely hindered me.

I would see other vloggers and bloggers getting brand work, paid opportunities, being taken to the Maldives on free trips, getting thousands for one mention in their video, winning awards . . . while I was sat in my bedroom at my mum's, with very little money, juggling my day job and YouTube, and trying to get the important issues out there. It felt that my followers got what I was trying to do – I have had a fab bunch of people right from the early days who I have built a real connection with – but the wider YouTube world didn't, and brands were not sure of me. They seemed to prefer the people who were fluffy, uncontroversial, and seemingly living a perfect life, no matter whether that was a true image or not.

It felt demoralising at times, but I was determined that what I was doing was right. My aim was – and is – about educating, raising awareness, and getting people to be strong enough to be who they are. To be brave enough to say that even if society's warped view of what is acceptable doesn't include me, well actually I am acceptable to me, and others' opinions should change. If I am OK with me, other people need to be too.

On my channel and my blog I am very clear that I don't talk about the latest food or fitness trend, as that doesn't matter to me. Instead I want people to come on and feel uplifted, inspired, happy and comforted. I want it to be the source of inspiration that I didn't have when I was growing up.

My amazing growing following always gave me great feedback, and made me believe I wasn't on my own with my vision. Plus it was also about direct results – the more I was able to help people, the more I felt sure I was doing the right thing. Every message from someone telling me they now saw themselves in a better light, or had worked out a way to deal with their problems, or simply felt they weren't alone because of something I had said, was incredible. It was just a case of breaking down the barriers that society had created for me, as well as the barriers I had made for myself.

Besides, it wasn't like I was completely turning my back on the area I had started out in. Conversations about make-up and fashion continued to be a part of my channel, as they are something that I love talking about. Putting outfits together is so much fun, as is putting on a great face of make-up. The difference was

I could literally live in a tracksuit with no make-up for the rest of my life and be perfectly happy, so fashion and beauty are both hobbies, whereas the women's issues and social taboos that I was beginning to tackle were not. These were a crucial part of life for me and other people, and if I was to make a real difference, that is where I was going to do it.

Let's face it, when I am long gone, I don't want to be yet another YouTuber who talked about MAC lipsticks and NARS palettes; I want to be remembered as way more than that. So I continued to push ahead with the refocused 'Ugly Face of Beauty', and kept brainstorming ideas for videos on self-love, body image and confidence. I got my friends and boyfriend involved as guests, I talked about everything from orgasms to online dating to foot fetishes to insecurities to drinks with the girls. The positive comments and increase in followers continued, and my energies and passion for the tasks increased ten-fold.

One area I really had to work on, though, was my relationship with social media. On so many levels I loved it – bloody lucky given it was a big part of my job! – but at other times it could be desperately toxic. The key thing is getting your perfect relationship with it right, so that it doesn't take over your life.

The online world has given me a zest for life that I didn't know was possible. It has given me a chance to be the person I always knew I could be. I have been accepted in a way I had never been accepted before, and I never feel lonely as I have all these people talking to me. I love it for the friendships I have made just sitting in my bedroom, and for the connections with people around the world I would never have been lucky enough to meet in real life.

While I may still have felt the odd one out amongst other YouTubers, I felt very much part of a larger family online. Connecting with people that I would never come across in everyday life is one of the best things about blogging. I realised that so many of us are connected by the issues we have gone through, rather than just our backgrounds.

I am thankful for the way my eyes are opened to events, opinions and ways of life I would otherwise never have come across, and of course I love it for the banter, the jokes, the motivational pictures and the funny videos! Let's face it, social media and YouTube have changed my life, so for that I am going to be forever grateful.

But wow, let's talk about the trolls. These angry, nasty people I don't even know, sending abuse to me from behind their screens like vitriolic, warped little weirdos. They are the worst kind of bullies.

When I first started making videos in my bedroom for fun, I had no idea how successful they were going to end up being. So when people are amazed that someone with my low self-esteem would put themselves out there to be judged . . . well, I didn't realise that would happen. When you first start out it is just about fun. You are happy when a video has been watched twenty times! But as my channel's popularity grew, the judgement grew. It was always so superficial. No one ever criticised my character or content, it was always about my appearance, and more specifically my weight.

I was forever being called fat, minging, ugly . . . I quickly learnt I had to develop a backbone and let it wash over me. But every now and then a comment would hit a nerve, or I would be feeling negative and vulnerable anyway, and open to attack.

I'm not sure if trolls don't realise just how damaging their comments can be to a person's mental health, or if they just don't care. Or maybe in their sad little lives, damaging another person really is the result they are after.

When I am feeling strong and receive a pathetic, nasty jibe someone has dreamt up to try and be personal or funny, then it doesn't mean shit. I just block and delete and it takes the power away from them and gets me back in control.

But at other times if I am already feeling low and dealing with body image issues and someone says I look fat or they don't like my outfit, it can be enough to bring out my anxiety. Girl trolls tend to be a lot worse than guys. Boys' comments are often so basic and unoriginal, I've heard it all before, but girls really know how to hurt. I think they upset me more as I think: 'Hold on, you know what it is like to be a woman and the pressures we are under to look a certain way, and yet you have just been a complete bitch. Why?'

There have been situations where a troll has upset me, and I've let those stupid little 140 characters ruin my whole day. We are all only human and if told something about ourselves that we are sensitive about anyway it is bound to tap into our insecurities. It is easy to say just ignore it and don't listen, but that is not in our nature, so I have certain things I will try and tell myself instead. Ultimately they are all about recognising that you are worthy of love no matter what you look like or what you have been through, and that the compassion you have for yourself is the most important, first and foremost. After that you need to remind yourself that these people don't really know you and even if you put all your life on social media, people still don't really know you inside and out. They don't know your favourite colour (gold), your favourite type of juice (orange), or whatever. I try and pull back and gain perspective on whether what that person says matters to me, especially when it comes to what I look like, and the reality is it doesn't matter one tiny freaking little bit.

Other times, if I am feeling in a low place, I won't open myself up to it and will simply have time away from social media. I'll turn off my phone and laptop, and go and see a friend or treat myself to something fun.

It's a different matter if I see comments I disagree with that aren't aimed directly at me. If it is something completely offensive or hate spreading I won't be able to resist replying. I feel it is important to reply and educate that person – or just tell them to shut the fuck up! If you know you aren't fanning the flames, then responding seems a better choice than letting racism, sexism or whatever it is slide. It does depend a bit on my mood, though – if I am on my period, I am a lot more likely to lose my fucking shit!

Let's face it, for every twat online, there are a hundred amazing others who want to positively engage. I teach, encourage and share with them, and they do the same for me, so no one ever feels alone. It is those 99 per cent of people that I am really focused on when I go on social media.

That said, I did have one particularly bad burn thanks to social media with my ex-best friend . . . Although I have to admit I was partly at fault and learnt a big lesson in how *not* to use social media.

To give you some background, I had met my friend in High Wycombe when we were thirteen. She wasn't at my school, but we would hang out together and had a lot in common such as a love of singing and dancing, clothes, make-up and food. We also bonded over the fact we were both unhappy with our weight.

We came as a pair as far as other people were concerned, and we had fun. To cut a long story very short, she caused me a lot of hurt, and yet still I stuck with her out of some misguided sense of loyalty. Looking back, I realise I never liked who I was when I was with her. That should have been a sign, and deep down I knew the friendship was wrong, but I completely ignored my intuition.

Then I began to learn about the body positive movement and became more confident in who I was. People like Callie and Danielle were showing me what a positive, two-way friendship could be like. I was working on being a better person and finally I decided I couldn't associate with her any more. She wasn't good for me, and I wasn't even sure I liked her.

Don't get me wrong, I wasn't an angel either, but that was just another reason to get out of there – she brought out the worst in me.

One night I had had a few drinks, then discovered something that pushed me over the edge. Then, ERROR! Out of pure anger and frustration, I tweeted about it.

I hold my hands up; I shouldn't have used my public platform to moan about what was a private matter. To spread negativity was wrong. But please remember, before I am a YouTuber, before I am Gracie Francesca, I am a normal human being who was very upset that someone I cared about and had given so much of myself to would let me down so badly. So I reacted without thinking and used Twitter as an outlet for my sadness and anger.

But wow, the backlash. She kicked straight back on Twitter, making out I was a bully, and suddenly thousands of people seemed to believe her over me. Not just mutual friends who told me they would never speak to me again, but all these people on social media. I was getting online hate, judged by people I didn't know, even death threats.

Things got really bad and eventually I escaped to Malta by myself for a week. I slept in my room for fifteen hours a day, and tried to get my head around everything. It felt I was at the centre of a witch hunt.

It affected me for months after as I was so shaken by it. In fact her name still sends a shiver down my spine so I guess it still affects me. Interestingly, though, a lot of the mutual friends who took her side at the time have come to me since and apologised, saying they have found out the truth.

People often ask me what happened but I haven't said anything about it until writing this book, and by now I have learnt that some things are best left unsaid. I hadn't wanted to reignite the flame of something that left me feeling pretty damn shit. But it was also the wake-up call I needed to a) sort myself out at the time in terms of my friendships and relationships, and b) to start trusting that intuition I had ignored about our friendship. So in that way, perhaps it all happened for a reason – the universe was telling me I was an idiot for not trusting my instincts!

Either way, there was one big fat lesson I took away from it – don't air your dirty laundry on social media!

My Top Rules for Using Social Media

- Remember that online anyone can pretend to be whoever they want to be, so not everything, or everyone, or the image they portray of their lives, is real. Maybe the person you are comparing yourself to or lusting after isn't really loving life, doesn't really own a yacht in the south of France, or isn't even a twenty-year-old guy.

- Social media is not a place to vent about matters that are private between you and a family member or friend. Keep it as a place to exchange news, support others, ask for help, and provide entertainment.

- You never know who could be reading your social media. Your teacher, boss, future boss, mum, or the neighbour down the road may be able to access it, so no matter how tight you think your privacy settings are, be aware of the impression you give.

- Make use of the blocking function. Whether that is to block negative people, or specific words that could offend you, make use of it. Also report offensive material to the admins – all social media has an easy click option to do this.

- Connect with positive people who you can learn from, and let the stories you come across inspire you to be a better person.

- If it all gets a bit too heavy, or you find you have become too dependent on checking social media every few minutes, detox from it. Even a day away focusing on other stuff can do your mind a world of good.

- Learn to make quick assessments of trolls. Report them if they deserve it, argue with them if you think you can make

> a difference, or mostly just delete, block and put them out of your mind as the worthless idiots they are.
> - Keep everything in perspective, see social media for what it is, and enjoy!

Then, three years after I started 'Ugly Face of Beauty', came one particular week in autumn 2014 where it felt that as if all my hard work had finally paid off. Where the hobby that began with a basic video on my twenty-first birthday and grew into a lot of hard work, fun, and something with real meaning, got some great recognition. It wasn't my main motivation for what I was doing, obviously, but I was seeing all these other people winning awards and being touted as the next big thing, and I was like, 'Oi, I want a piece of that!'

One of the big awards at the time was the *Cosmopolitan* Blog Awards, as they were one of the first publications to really get on board and realise the value of the online scene. They had awards that recognised all sorts of areas such as fashion, beauty, lifestyle and travel. Followers nominated you and I found myself up for the Next Newcomer title, and then the voting began.

I was invited to the awards party at the Oxo Tower in London, a lovely fancy awards night with cocktails and food. And then the announcements came, and I had won! I was so happy and emotional about it. It felt like my vision for my role in the blogging world was being validated, that people were acknowledging I *was* doing something worthwhile. Like anything in life, your passion for it can keep you going, but recognition can be like the icing on the cake.

The next morning I met with a management company called AAA who signed me up as a client, with the aim of helping me develop my career. It felt like people were finally believing in me and understanding my vision. It was such a big week for me!

Why You Should Celebrate Yourself

We live in a world where it is more acceptable to be insecure than it is to celebrate yourself. Think about it. When did you last say to your friend: 'I wrote a brilliant essay last night, I'm actually quite good at this subject.' Or: 'I came up with some really creative ideas at work today, the boss is going to be very happy.' Or: 'I look shit-hot in this dress!'

The reality is more: 'My essay was rubbish, I think I'm going to fail.' Or: 'My ideas in work are so poor, I'm worried I'll get the sack.' Or: 'Argh, my arms look so fat in this dress.' See what I mean?

For whatever reason, people seem to understand insecurities more. They get it if you feel unhappy with your body, feel depressed, or are worried you are having a fat day. They don't get it if you are loving who you are, feeling confident and positive. Sometimes they don't even like it. It's as though there is a guilt or a shame in being proud of who you are and showing off your achievements, and people think you are being conceited or up yourself.

Well, screw 'em . . . I celebrate everything! Good work meeting? Cocktails with the friends. Nice comments on a blog post? Out for dinner. I revel in the feeling, because nothing beats the sense of being proud of yourself. We all need to celebrate ourselves and our achievements. A feeling of achievement nurtures your soul and feels good and can also give you the drive and the strength to do the greater things. Small achievements can lead to big success.

By small, I mean just whatever size feels right to you and the point you are in in life. When I was at my lowest and so depressed I didn't want to do a thing, I would celebrate getting out of bed. Yes, it was the smallest of things, but in the world I was existing in at that time, it was a massive achievement.

You don't have to be Beyoncé to celebrate who you are, because the journey that Beyoncé has had isn't what everyone is going to have. Your life was meant for you, and no one else has control over it, so what you make of it is up to you.

So next time you achieve something, no matter how small, make sure you think about treating yourself in some way. You need to realise that small things matter, and you are good enough.

After signing with AAA I threw myself into my channel with renewed energy, and the harder I worked, the more I saw results. The only problem was that this meant sitting on social media through the night, and creating videos when I could hardly keep my eyes open. It was getting too much alongside the day job, because I was still working in the kids' home full time.

I stood back and reassessed my life. My channel kept having to take second place because after a twenty-four-hour shift with very demanding kids – even if they weren't trying to be, they inevitably were – I wasn't always on form to tackle it. So I had to make a decision to do one or the other, which was scary, when it felt my entire future and my mental health was at stake. I was very factual about it. OK, Grace, this work in the care home is the best job of your life, and you love it. But where are you heading long-term? You become a senior care assistant, which is where I was headed at that time, then deputy manager, then manager. But even then you are never your own boss, you are always – to put it bluntly – going to be someone's bitch, as there is always a company who owns and oversees the care home, and therefore effectively they are the real manager.

I realised for me that wasn't enough. My brain was buzzing with business ideas combined with ways I could help other people who had gone through crap in their lives like I had. I was getting more and more excited about where all of this could go. If I combined my work experience and training with my own life experiences and my already growing YouTube channel I could have something really unique and exciting here. I would be helping other people while doing a job I loved. So I handed my notice in, and bam, that was it. By January 2015 I was a full-time influencer.

So then commenced the year of amazing breakfasts and posh drinks! Otherwise known as meeting people and getting my face out there. I had as many meetings with brands as I could, and went to events and launches at every opportunity. I worked relentlessly on my YouTube videos and social media, and made sure that I was a 24/7 online presence, and chatted with other people who I hoped I could learn from.

Finally I began to get a few paid jobs here and there, firstly doing a beauty box thing for a beauty brand, and then for E45 cream. They led to a few more, and after that things just kept growing. It felt as though at last my timing was right. The world was becoming more open to the idea of plus-sized fashion and the need for models of all sizes. Body positivity campaigns were springing up, and people were beginning to discuss diversity and mental health. It was as though all the stuff I had been discussing for years was suddenly 'a big thing' and I was no longer a lone voice. Sometimes it felt as though celebs who knew nothing about the issues were jumping on the bandwagon to chat about mental health etc. That was annoying in one way as they didn't really know what they were talking about, but at the same time it was good as it was yet another way to raise awareness. Because of these changes it was as though suddenly it was like I ticked all the boxes for these brands, and I was being sought after for my opinion and asked to take part in shoots and campaigns.

People were wising up to the lack of diversity across the media, and looking at ways they could change that to appeal to more customers. My workload shot up, and I did a campaign for Evans, and a six-page spread for *Cosmo*. The snowball effect was happening, where the more work I got, the more work that led to. It was amazing, and exactly what I had been hoping for. I started to become a key person at the forefront of these important social issues. My dreams were finally beginning to fall into place!

At the same time it was a great confidence boost for me in confirming that the message I had been trying to put out there was the right one. That pushing on my own for those few years when everyone else had been focused on fashion and beauty had been worth it. There was an audience who needed to hear the messages I was putting out there. I was building the foundations for the 'me' that I hoped would continue for years to come.

One of the most common things that people said about me in the comments on my posts or on social media was that I was 'like a big sister' to them. The advice, realness and openness was what they were after, and a few people started dubbing me the 'Internet's Big Sister'. The name totally touched me and I loved the idea. It really fitted with what I wanted to do, and I kept that thought in my mind from then on – give the advice that you would have liked to have heard from the big sister you never had.

I am also always so careful to be honest. Yes, I want everything I say to be positive and inspirational, but life isn't always like that. So when I have been going through a bad time or hate how I look, I am honest with my followers about it. There is no point pretending, or that takes away the validity of everything else I say. It is important to recognise your own thoughts and recognise that they are there, even if you choose not to listen to them. So that honesty is as much for me as for those who I hope are looking up to me.

DON'T Fake It Until You Make It

I love a good saying, but not all of them are good. Far from it, in fact, as there are quite a few that can confirm negative stereotypes or plant exactly the wrong kind of idea in someone's mind.

My most hated one is 'Fake it until you make it'. What? Why on earth would you do that? This is a really stupid bit of advice.

I feel like this advice is setting you up to fail before you have even begun. Rather than tackling what you really need to do to make it, it is encouraging you to just pretend. Don't learn, admit where you need help, tackle the issues; no, just fake it.

But as far as I am concerned no matter what make-up you put on, what sassy outfit, what confident body language you try and give off, if it is all a façade hiding the issues beneath, well, you may get by like that for a bit, but you will eventually fail.

If under that façade you are unhappy, unmotivated, lacking confidence, haven't a clue what you are doing, whatever it is, it will be exposed when the façade drops away. Then you are screwed! So be real. There's no point faking it, you *won't* make it! Instead own your feelings, push your boundaries and ask for help – that's the path to success!

A year after winning Next Newcomer at the *Cosmopolitan* Blog Awards, I won their Best Vlog award for the 'Ugly Face of Beauty', which was amazing. I was totally overwhelmed and couldn't quite believe it. The awards equalled more press, and more press equalled more work, and things just kept on growing. People started to talk about me as a brand, which was kind of weird, but cool too, as it was more confirmation of the fact I was succeeding.

The most incredible award I have ever won was the Most Inspiring Role Model award at *InStyle* magazine's Project 13 Blog Awards. I got so emotional over that one and was half crying, half laughing. What a great feeling that is, to be called an inspiring role model. It was what I really hoped I was being, but it was the best feeling to have it confirmed by a third party.

Since then I have been called that lots of times, but each time still really touches me and kind of inspires me to go on and do more role-model type things!

I love that women are much more supportive of each other now, and when they see someone do something they think is great, they tell them and let them know they are a role model, rather than trying to pull them down.

There have been some standout people who I look up to, who have made me feel amazing with their compliments, such as Charlotte Tilbury, incredible make-up artist and girl boss, who invited me to a dinner she was hosting. I was so excited to go, as I love her work. But it turned out the feeling was mutual. She told me: 'Grace, I love that you have kicked back against all the stuff that tells people they are not good enough in what they are doing with their lives. You are very empowering for younger people today, and I wish there were more people like you. You inspire me, you really do.'

Bloody hell, that was mental. Hello, this is Charlotte Tilbury telling *me* that I inspire *her*?!

Another brilliant famous person who I see as a role model now and who incredibly said the same about me is Alesha Dixon. We actually come from very similar backgrounds, and have a lot of the same tastes and thoughts on things. I met her when a brand she was working with asked me to do a video and we got on really well. I told her my story and she said: 'You are amazing, it is an honour to be on your channel,' which was so nice to hear! She has been massively supportive, as has Katie Piper who is a truly inspirational woman. We met at a fashion event and then kept in touch. Her focus is obviously dealing with facial disfigurement and scarring, but I think ultimately everything we both talk about leads to the same message about being confident with who you are, having self-belief and focusing on self-love.

Holly from *Geordie Shore* is another person who really stuck out in my mind for being such a babe when we met, but also for her honesty. She told me that she had really struggled with body image over the years and loved that I was talking about all the topics that had previously been taboo. She said: 'I think it is great that you talk about cellulite and stretchmarks, as I didn't have that when I was younger. It is so important for people to accept themselves for who they are, but when there is no one showing you how to do that, you can end up getting yourself in a right mess.'

She told me that she has particularly suffered with body image issues since being on television and that she feels the pressure to look a certain way. She was a lot bigger than she is now when she came into the public eye and I think it is sad that she felt the need to conform to be successful, but I understand it. It is very hard to be that celebrity who can say, 'No, I don't care what people say, I can put up with the insanely negative and bitchy comments when I'm pictured in the media in my bikini.'

Holly said: 'For just one day I wish I didn't feel this way about my body, and that I could be happy with who I am.' It made me sad to hear it, but I also got it completely. No matter how much I talk about body positivity and loving yourself, and even with all the work I have done on myself to make that a reality for me, I still have days when I don't feel like I am good enough. But all you can do is keep trying to change the way you think, and keep questioning the way society makes you feel you need to look and act a certain way. If there is one message I try to get across to my followers more than any it is constantly reiterating that there is more to life than the figure on the scales or the number on your clothes label. You are so much more than what you look like.

At the same time I keep searching out new role models for myself. Every day I see people who are absolutely inspiring, being a bad ass, or a total girl boss. People who show me what can happen when you work on yourself and accept yourself. The internet and social media, when used the right way, is so empowering. I wouldn't be on it if I didn't feel that, but these women are my reason to be there.

Social media has allowed me to explore stories from other places and see all sorts of people make a real success of themselves. All over the world are people whose faces don't traditionally fit, who still got to where they wanted to be.

The more time I have spent on the internet, the more I have seen the world. I have seen the kind of people make it that I didn't see in my home town as I was growing up, and it has been so inspiring. People I'd never have known about without the internet, but who now make me happy and motivated.

The worrying thing is, despite the fact that within a few short years vlogging has become a booming industry with certain influencers seen as the next celebrities, the lack of diversity within that has become ever more apparent. The word 'influencers' came about because of just how much influence certain YouTube stars can have on young people. Vloggers are no longer a handful of slightly eccentric people sitting in their bedrooms recording stuff; vlogging is now a very mainstream, so it is even more important for a range of people to be shown, sending out the right positive messages.

I often talk about the fact that girls like me want to see girls like me win. The truth is it is not just about 'want', it is actually a desperate need for it. People who are different need to be seen to succeed, to inspire the next generation. I don't just mean in the creative arts but in all inspirational roles, whether that is banking, science or YouTube, because right now, they are still too few and far between.

I find it weird even now to be called a role model, but it is a position I take very seriously. I am not perfect, in fact I am far from it! But it is my honesty about those flaws, and the positives that come out of sharing them, that I hope always helps and inspires people.

That is why it is important for me to tell my story, to talk about my childhood and where I am from. I got out of that world of crime, poverty and sadness. I made it out, and people still stuck there need to see that, so they know they can do it too. Come on, ladies, don't be held back, you can do whatever you want to do if you just believe in yourselves!

People I Look up to Today

I think the fact I felt I had no one to look up to when I was kid and now I have a huge list shows how quickly things are changing and improving. Back in the day, my lovely RS teacher Mary McCrystal was practically holding the fort on her own!

Here are just a few people I see as my role models. They are curvy and skinny, black and white, young and old, rich and poor. But with all of them there is something I can relate to and admire. They all give me ideas about things I am capable of, and how I can be a better person.

- **Michelle Obama:** This woman is unfuckingbelievable! I mean who the hell doesn't look up to Michelle? She is like this amazing person who has done so much not just for women of colour, or all women, but society as a whole. It kind of feels like the world is a better place because of her and her husband. A strong, moral woman in a perfect partnership!

- **Gabi Fresh/Gabi Greg:** The American version of me! Curvy, big curly hair, blogger, feminist and designer.

- **The Body Posi Panda:** This girl is great. She is called Megan and has become a good friend of mine. She is a recovered anorexic, and does so much to bring awareness to body issues and body positivity, and basically wants to get everyone to love themselves and their figures in such an upbeat way. Check her out!

- **Michaela Coel:** A great actress from East London. She battled against the odds to become a successful singer-songwriter, poet and playwright, and then starred in her own show *Chewing Gum* on E4 which won her a BAFTA.

- **Doreen Lawrence:** Another woman who has shown incredible strength. As the mum of Stephen Lawrence she has never given up the battle to seek justice for her son.

- **The Slumflower:** Chidera is a young black girl from London who has done really well for herself. She does a lot of public speaking and blogs about self-love.

Chapter 11
STOP WALLOWING IN SELF-PITY

'Two things to remember in life: take care of your thoughts when you are alone, and take care of your words when you are with other people.'

I hate London Fashion Week. Somehow I knew before I even got there that it would be a place where all the bits of fashion that I don't like would come together. Models all of the same body type, i.e. size eight and under, unaffordable high-end fashion, and everything you see on films that mocks the fashion world and makes it out as shallow, bitchy and fake. It is not at all like the fashion world that I love and inhabit on a daily basis, where I like it to be inclusive, high-street, open-minded, friendly, and fun.

Sadly my fears were 100 per cent spot on. Everyone was judging each other on appearances and outfits, and there was a LOT of serious attitude, with people trying to prove they were better than everyone else. Honestly, it was not my scene at all. Don't get me wrong, you all know I love 'fashunn with a passion'! But for me, London Fashion Week is just a total turn-off. As far as I am concerned it needs a total overhaul . . .

Having said all that, I have now been twice, and they were two very different experiences. The first time was in September 2015, when I was there in my first proper presenting job. I had been wanting to try my hand at presenting for a while, and incredibly I was asked to cover LFW for the BBC. I couldn't believe I was being handed this amazing opportunity and couldn't wait to get stuck in.

I found some bits of LFW unexpectedly positive during the filming, one of which was the designers. I had assumed they would all be stuck up and acting like they were better than everyone else, but actually those that I did interview were fantastic, great fun, and really quite modest. I also loved the hectic, excited vibe backstage, with everyone running around manically focused on their task, whether it was steaming a dress or finding a make-up brush. It was exactly how I imagined backstage would be, and although I felt a bit in the way, it was an exciting experience.

The final result was a programme called *LFW: Grace Victory's Top Picks* and I was so proud of it. It was difficult work filming the show, but I loved it. We were shooting for hours on end, redoing scenes, and I constantly had to look alert and happy, but I learnt so much, and they were a great crew.

Then, in February 2016, I had my first official invite to it as me, rather than because I was there for the BBC, and despite my concerns I was really, really excited. It was a nod to the fact I was being taken seriously as an influencer, and it was a great way to get a glimpse of trends that would be hitting the high street down the line. I was also getting all the treatment thrown in, not to mention the fact my best friend Callie Thorpe and I had a complimentary suite in the ME Hotel, a gorgeous five-star hotel on The Strand. Result! The place was amazing and properly posh.

But sadly, despite all of these amazing things, I wasn't in a good place mentally. I had had a shit Christmas with all sorts of trauma going on, it looked like a break-up with my boyfriend Simon was on the cards, and I had gone through a horrific falling-out with a friend. I was feeling emotionally unstable, and my anxiety was kicking in with force. That is the thing with mental health problems, you can be in what should be the most perfect place in the world, and your mind can still do its own thing to destroy it. I hated the way I looked and wasn't comfortable in my outfits, and as a result I felt like I was taking it out on other people and being a bitch to everyone around me.

Then Callie and I went to a show by a Russian brand that I'd not heard of before, but my PR had booked us onto the front row with some of her other clients, such as radio presenter Pandora Christie and model Caprice, and we went to see what it was all about. As we sat ourselves down in our allocated seats, and began looking around, a woman working for the brand came over and said to me and Callie: 'If you two would like to move to this other row instead, I have found you better seats, and you will be closer to the cameras.'

I stared at her. I couldn't believe what I was hearing. Err, hello, the cameras were obviously going to be on the front row! She stared back at me, firm in her determination that we would move. Thoughts were rushing through my mind, and all I could think was that she wanted to move us for the way we looked. She thought we were too fat for the front row.

My face was burning with embarrassment, and with no other choice without making a scene, we followed her to our new seats. I was seething inside and wanted to scream at this stupid bitch of a woman! No way was I giving this horrific no-mark brand any coverage in my blogs about the week. Callie and I sat in silence through the show, and as I calmed down, my anger turned to sadness. I could hardly take in what any of the models were doing. I had been kicked off the front row at a London Fashion Week show for being fat. Wow. If my sadness and inse-curities weren't already high enough, this cemented them. Yet again I wasn't good enough the way I was. In retrospect, Callie and I were the most stylish people at that show #justsaying but I wasn't in a place mentally to have the strength of character to deal with it at that time.

Back at the hotel I had a complete breakdown. I was crying and sobbing, and while Callie was also upset over our treatment, she was horrified at the way I was reacting. As she tried to calm me down she got upset too, then eventually demanded: 'What the fuck is going on with you?'

I talked about all the shit that had been happening in my life in the last couple of months, and at the end waited for her sym-pathy. She had been brilliant support in the previous months in building up my confidence and getting me to see I was fine as I was. Surely she would do this again now.

Callie took a deep breath, then carefully said: 'When I felt like this a few years ago, my friends told me to stop wallowing in self-pity, and I am going to tell that to you right now.'

Say what? I stared at her, taken aback. Did she really think that was helpful? 'What a shit friend you are!' I stuttered.

We got through the rest of LFW, still as the closest of friends, but I suppose I harboured a bit of hurt over her comments. It was only over the next few days, weeks, even months, that I began to understand what she meant and why she had said it. It gave me the kick up the arse to sort myself out that I needed. I realised I had been wallowing in the depressive world I was used to living in, concentrating on all the negative thoughts and bad things in my life. But it was like a big dark hole – the more I thought like that, the deeper I was sinking into it, and unless I consciously fought to pull myself out of it, I was never going to escape.

It was such an important lesson and I'm really grateful to Callie for being brave enough to call me out. Fight for what you want, what you believe in, for the life you know deep down that you deserve, and soon things become clearer, the clouds of doom start to fade, and the light starts to come back in.

I think this is one of the best bits of advice I have ever been given. So I give it to other people occasionally now too, when I can see that they need it the way I did. Don't get me wrong, sometimes you 100 per cent need a period of time to deal with the shit that life is throwing at you. You need to curl up in that dark place, think negative things, and cry. But once you start to feel comfortable in that dark place, when you embrace it too readily and weirdly almost feel happy there, then you know in your gut that it is time to move on. You are starting to get stuck in that place when really if you are going to heal yourself, you need to get back up.

Forget about festering in unhappiness just because you have got used to it and start striving for a better life. Get your shit together, face up to your issues or any adversities getting in your way. And if you need a friend to give you that kick up the arse then so be it. Obviously this doesn't apply if you are in the depth of mental health issues, but other times we are just wallowing, and sometimes we all need that encouragement to dig deep and realise we do have strength and courage in us to move onwards and upwards.

P.S. As for London Fashion Week, you can kiss my fat arse!

Chapter 12
CLEAN EATING'S DIRTY SECRETS

'Mirror, mirror on the wall
You seem to think you know it all
Why do, why do I believe?'
JoJo

In Spring 2016, I was approached on Twitter by a researcher from the production company True Vision, as they wanted to see if I would be interested in presenting a documentary they were in the process of getting commissioned for BBC3. Called *Clean Eating's Dirty Secrets*, it instantly caught my attention as I had been watching the clean eating culture for a while, and wondering if it wasn't just the latest diet fad that was taking over from the likes of the more obvious dieting routes such as WeightWatchers and Slimming World.

In theory I believe it started out as a positive way of eating – the original idea was to eat lots of wholefoods in a kind of back-to-nature way, cutting down on foods that have been overly processed and eating more 'real' foods, so veg, fruit, nuts, proteins, etc. But even the name implies that any other food is 'dirty' and so it began to make people feel pressure about what they could and couldn't eat. It was also clear that, over time, people jumping on the clean-eating bandwagon weren't just treating it as a positive way of eating, but were adding more and more lists of food to the banned pile, opening the door for more restrictive diets. My instinct was to dislike the whole concept, as once again it seemed to me the focus was ultimately all on how thin a person could be, no matter how much they were trying to dress it up as being 'kind to your body'. I also liked the idea of exploring orthorexia (see below) and its links to clean eating, as it was an eating disorder I had never heard of, even though I try to be pretty clued up on mental health and disordered eating as a whole.

What Are all these Eating Disorders?

- **Eating disorder:** When someone develops disturbed and destructive behaviours and thoughts related to food. This can be:

- **Anorexia:** Lack or loss of appetite for food (as a medical condition). An emotional disorder characterised by an obsessive desire to lose weight, by refusing to eat.

- **Bulimia:** An emotional disorder characterised by a distorted body image and an obsessive desire to lose weight, in which bouts of extreme overeating are followed by fasting or self-induced vomiting or purging.

- **Binge eating:** Episodes of uncontrollable eating, where excessive amounts are eaten quickly.

- **Orthorexia:** An obsession with eating foods that one considers healthy. A medical condition where the sufferer systematically avoids specific foods that they believe to be harmful.
- **Disordered eating:** When what we would determine as 'normal' eating patterns become disrupted.

Presenting this documentary would obviously be a great opportunity career-wise, and it was encouraging when the producers told me they had watched my LFW presenting and been impressed by it. I guess that had become like a mini online show-reel for me and I did a little secret celebration dance to hear that. I couldn't believe how much my life had moved on just one year after I had become a full-time influencer. I left my first meeting with the production company thinking yup, absolutely, this job is for me, and luckily the BBC3 commissioner gave it the go-ahead and agreed I was the right person to present it. Contracts were signed and off we went . . .

Filming began almost instantly and the idea was I would try out various so-called clean eating diets and talk to some of the key people within the movement, and those in the know about orthorexia too. I was interested to explore a plant-based diet – effectively a vegan diet – as it was getting so much coverage at the time. When it came down to it, though, I liked some of the food like the smoothies, and some of the pastries, but God, it was a lot of effort. I understand why people would choose to go down that route for ethical reasons, but I didn't agree with the people who were on a plant-based diet just for the health purposes and trying to push it on to others as the right way to eat. As for raw vegans . . . don't get me started! I was so moody when I was on that diet, as it just took all the fun out of food. Meals are meant to be pleasurable, a nice experience, but that just felt like a constant battle. I couldn't eat anything I wanted or liked, and the constant thinking ahead and spending a lot of time preparing meals just didn't fit with my lifestyle. It was an incredibly restrictive way to eat, and I couldn't help but suspect that if you were prone to disordered eating, this type of diet would definitely appeal. Eventually I was like, nah, why am I putting myself through this? I'm done!

I tried several other diets, including a high starch diet where I had to do a potato cleanse, living off . . . you guessed it, nothing but potatoes. I mean come on, it was totally ridiculous; even with the most basic nutritional knowledge I could tell that wasn't healthy. It seemed like the focus was being restrictive for the sake of it, rather than for a health reason. It was so traumatic that there was no way my stress levels from attempting to follow all these diets weren't giving me more health problems than eating a big greasy burger would have! I just couldn't believe any of these diets were healthy.

As filming continued, I was horrified by some of the people I was meeting who were advocating these diets, some of which were very extreme and restrictive. Hardly any of them had any qualifications to set themselves up in this field; instead they had just decided to declare themselves experts. As soon as I put any difficult questions to them with scientific facts – provided by a dietician, not myself – they would refuse to answer, or try to move the topic away. It felt like these girls were honestly more like modern-day witch doctors, seeing if they could get money out of a gullible audience.

They all seemed to be thin, middle/upper-class white girls with long swishy hair, and the attitude was very much 'eat like me and you might be lucky enough to look like me'. There was a real sense of superiority to it; if you only ate the same diet as them, you could join their club. They really sell the idea of 'the cleaner you eat, the healthier, happier and hotter you will be!' but to me it was bullshit. It was all about controlled eating and restriction. It was the diet culture of old, but packaged differ-ently, although once again aimed at women and playing on their insecurities. A negative message dressed up under the veil of positivity that had the potential to be extremely damaging.

I particularly didn't buy into the idea that this way of eating was about health. I had my blood and pee tested as part of the show and came back healthy, despite my weight. Yet up close some of those 'experts' were anything but. They had brittle nails, dry hair and unhealthy skin under the make-up. I honestly believed that a lot of them were undernourished.

One of the specialists I spoke to on *Clean Eating's Dirty Secrets* was a therapist called Emmy Brunner, Director at a treatment centre called The Recover Clinic. She was really interesting, and I was shocked when she told me that they had treated or heard from at least a third of the top bloggers in the country. Should people suffering eating disorders really be setting themselves up as diet experts?

All the research that went into the documentary hammered home to me that the issue for many people is their lack of belief in their ability to eat moderately. People are so afraid of putting on weight that they go the other way and overly control their eating. So-called clean eating is just a way to have more power over your diet, and a list of instructions to follow strictly to make yourself feel more in control, but it doesn't matter if you are fat or thin, undereating or overeating – obsessive eating patterns of any sort are not OK. As with most things in life, moderation is clearly key. In most cases there is no need to cut out gluten, sugar or whatever it is completely, just eat it in moderation.

At the end of filming I talked to a genuinely experienced qualified dietician who told me that as far as she was concerned the Mediterranean-style diet is the healthiest. That was it – a simple, balanced, lifelong way of eating, that doesn't cut out anything and focuses on fresh, healthy food. Who could have guessed it?

When the documentary aired, it got an incredible response. So many people contacted me to say they had developed eating problems after trying to follow one of the so-called clean eating diets. They had been so obsessed with following the various rules that eating had become all about control, not about fuel and enjoyment. The show was a huge hit and became the most downloaded BBC3 show ever to have been shown on BBC iPlayer. I had learnt a huge amount and this had been a brilliant boost to my presenting career.

Sadly, though, making the documentary had opened up my own issues with eating again. I think I secretly knew before we started filming that it mightn't be the best thing for my mental health, but I wanted to do it so badly. The combination of raising awareness and the presenting job was too important to me to turn it down. But given that I already had a track record of a pretty messed-up relationship with food, this unsurprisingly made things worse.

Before filming, I felt like I was generally in a much better place than I had been just a year or so before, thanks in main to the influence of the Body Positive movement. I was less weight-obsessed, and had tried to stop thinking about what every meal contained, what exactly each mouthful was doing to my body, and just enjoy it for what it was. But this programme needed me to do the opposite and entirely focus on what I ate. So although the end message that we were giving to viewers was exactly the right one as far as I was concerned, going through the process made some of my old thoughts and habits reappear.

Body image issues started rearing their head again, and I decided that I needed to do a strong video in an attempt to help me try and tackle them, and I mean *really* tackle them, head on. The resulting video was called 'Naked'. In it I talk about taking away everything I am on the outside and everything I do, and facing the issues that make me feel naked. I did all the visuals and went back to my family home and filmed myself naked, focusing on the rolls, stretchmarks, uneven skin tones, marks and darker areas.

I played a song over the top called 'I Am' by JoJo, which is about someone struggling with the image they see of themselves in the mirror, and questioning whether they are worthy of love.

It was so hard to make, and I felt so vulnerable – naked, essentially – in the video. But it got a lot of support and positive comments and, most incredibly of all, JoJo got in touch to show her support for the video all across her social media which was amazing.

I felt temporarily buoyed by the responses, but I knew deep down it was never going to be an answer to these stupid body image issues that I just never seemed to be able to rid myself of. That solution appeared in a different way . . .

During filming, Emmy from The Recover Clinic pulled me to one side. She is a clinician as well as Director and she suggested that it might be a good idea for me to go and see her to discuss my own eating once the documentary was finished. While everyone else involved in the show thought I was doing fine, she was clearly able to see the demons I was struggling with.

I agreed and went to see her, thinking we were just going to have a bit of a chat, she might clear a few things up for me, and we would be done, nice-knowing-her type of thing. I couldn't have been more wrong.

Emmy and I talked about food, and I told her I was weird as my weight was always up and down, and I am always trying to lose weight and be thinner. I explained how I swing between restricting and binge eating, and told her about my childhood and self-harm. She asked a few questions, but was mostly writing notes. At the end of the assessment she concluded that I have quite a complex eating disorder, where I have an anorexic mind, but that it plays out in overeating. So I almost hear anorexic voices, but they manifest in other ways such as bingeing or making myself sick. It is not simple-sounding, I realise, and not many people get it, but it is apparently tightly tied in with suppressing childhood trauma, and well . . . If you have been keeping up with the book so far, you will know I had plenty to suppress!

Emmy also diagnosed me as having post traumatic stress disorder – PTSD – effectively confirming that what I was going through was caused by earlier trauma.

As with the first time I had gone to counselling, it was nice to have a diagnosis, as it was like an explanation for what was going on in my head, and somehow that makes it less scary, it normalises it. It was also a more specific diagnosis than the first time when I was just told I had an eating disorder, so it was quite an eye-opener. It became clear I had never really properly acknowledged what my eating disorders had been or what the causes of them could be.

As I talked with Emmy about it, I kept saying, 'I'm just really weird, I would …' or 'I would feel like . . . as I am weird!' She flagged up that it was my favourite way to describe myself and my eating, as though I knew there was something not quite right about it but I was never willing to give it a stronger description or medical term.

The more we talked the more it became apparent that I secretly believed all the incorrect stereotypes people have about eating disorders. Fat people can't have an eating disorder. Therefore I had just assumed I was being dramatic to even consider I'd had a disorder at all and really it was just me not having my shit together. Oh dear, Grace …

This meant, effectively, that I didn't fully acknowledge that I had gone through anorexia, bulimia and binge eating at various stages in my life until I was in my mid-twenties – thirteen years after it first became a serious issue. How mad is that? More must be done to make sure young people are given the help they need when they need it.

Of course, Emmy didn't let me just come in for that one quick chat and before I knew it I was having weekly sessions with her focusing on holistic therapy treatment for my childhood traumas. Emmy could see that my mental health wasn't in the best place because of everything that I had locked up in a tiny little box, hidden away in the depths of my brain. She taught me that these thoughts would come spilling out at times when I could least control them, impacting on things such as my desire to binge eat. I would cope with the negative thoughts by eating, but then the guilt of eating and putting on weight would make me feel bad, and I would eat again to deal with that . . . how's that for a great cycle!

Emmy gave me tasks to do in between our sessions as therapy and recovery is something you need to really work at. It doesn't work to just turn up at your weekly session and expect that to fix you. The tasks would go back to a real base point, as though I was needed to repair myself from the ground upwards. For example I would have to spend the week 'thinking kind thoughts', 'being kinder to myself', etc. You think that sounds easy, but unless your head is in the right place, it's really hard.

Emmy taught me in the sessions that trying to make my body better in the hope that my mind would follow was the wrong way round. Sooner or later, my mind was going to fuck it up.

You need to get your mind in order, then your body will follow.

This is such a simple bit of advice, yet one that so few people actually follow. If there is one thing I would like readers to take away from this book into their own life, this is it! When your mind is in a good place, your body will find the weight it should naturally be. This may not be super skinny, but whatever that weight is, you need to accept it, maintain a healthy mind-set, and love yourself, whether you are big, small, or somewhere in between, no matter what.

As I write this I am twenty-six years old and still in therapy. I am a work in progress, which is no bad thing, as I think we all always are really. But my mind still has some bits to deal with before I feel like I will be completely at peace with my issues with food and how I perceive myself, and that translates into my weight. I am confident that when I am mentally 100 per cent, my body will follow.

Interestingly, The Recover Clinic has a 100 per cent success rate for people who graduate from the treatment programme, so there has to be something to it. Don't just tackle your eating, work on your brain too.

Emmy's sessions didn't half open up a can of worms, though. My anxiety kicked in full force, and it was clear that this was one of those situations where things had to get worse before they could get better. You know that saying, 'ignorance is bliss'? Well, sometimes I wished I was still ignorant! When I was very young and going through all this crap and not realising it wasn't OK, I just got on with it. Or at least it felt like I did, just cracking on in my own way. In reality, everything was getting bottled up subconsciously and I wasn't aware of it. It was only when I went into therapy that I could face it straight on. It was like I woke up and saw a lot of stuff that I had known inside me, but hadn't had to deal with until that point, and quite frankly, facing it was hellish.

We talked about my dad and my friends and all the abandonment issues that came with them. We discussed my sister, and
my fucked-up family, and general life experiences. But actually
the hardest sessions turned out to be about my mum. While my
anger at Dad is very one-dimensional – 'you weren't there' being
the gist of it – with Mum it came out that I placed a lot of blame
on her. Because I felt I had to look after myself and protect her,
and because of the pressure that came with our childhood that
pushed us to grow up fast, it emerged I resented her for. I was
quite shocked by this but apparently it is common for a child to
place the greater blame on the person who was actually there. I
was conflicted by those sessions, as it wasn't something I wanted
to feel and I wasn't even sure it was fair, but you can't change
your own emotions, I guess.

I would get home from the sessions and often cry for hours. I
found my brain would try to forget the sessions, and I would
have to write down what we had discussed.

They were so hard that I often didn't want to go, but that is
where Emmy was good. She would call and pester me – 'make
sure I see you tomorrow!' – and I knew I would go really, because
as much as I hated it, I felt she got me, and if I was ever to become
a better, stronger person, getting all this shit out once and for all
had to be a good thing.

I am still seeing her weekly eight months on, but we must
be getting there, as the memories feel a lot more ordered, and I
have definitely worked through and dealt with a lot of them. I
think writing this book has actually been an extension of the
therapy – getting my thoughts and understanding of myself
in order.

Emmy's Top Tips on Dealing with Disordered Eating

- Make sure that you seek advice from a specialist professional.

- There is nothing wrong with you; *you* are not weird (Grace's favourite word). You have an illness that can be treated and healed.

- Start keeping a journal or drawing as a way of connecting with how you feel.

- Try to recognise that any voice you hear in your head that tells you to hurt yourself is not a voice to be trusted.

- Try to practise acts of kindness toward yourself and others.

- Be mindful about what you are exposing yourself to online. There are lots of pro recovery and positive body image sites out there. This is what you need to be looking at.

- Have faith! Believe you can get well and you will!

Generally we don't talk about food or eating during the therapy sessions – I have started seeing a dietician so those conversations are saved for her – but with Emmy we focus on the idea that my trauma is playing out in food, and if we deal with the trauma the food issues won't be there. We have touched on the odd bit of food advice though that has been relevant to me, and one of them was a total revelation! I didn't even know what 'conscious eating' meant when it was first discussed, and I think it is crucial knowledge, so I want to share it with you!

Basically, I have always assumed that everyone else views food and choosing what to eat like I do . . . Well, I was wrong. My theory was that slim people must constantly watch what they eat and calorie count all the time, restricting their food intake to stay the same size, while overweight people must constantly overindulge. Well, that is just not true.

When I first mentioned this to Emmy, she was like, 'Erm no, Grace, when I go out to the shops to get lunch, I think, "What do I fancy today?" Then I buy that, and that is where it ends.'

I stared at her, thinking of all the obsessing I did over it, the restricting, the calorie counting, the bingeing, the thinking about it from first to last minute of the day, and knew that I just really wanted to think like her.

Conscious eating is apparently what normal people with healthy eating habits do. It means listening to your body and hearing it tell you what you want to eat. That sounds simplistic, but imagine if you put ten plates of food in a room with a toddler. They would pick at that food all day when they got hungry, and would mix it up literally depending on what they fancied, and what their body told them they needed. So one hour they might choose the fruit pastilles and Cadbury Milky Stars, but the next they might pick the broccoli and apple. The child is going by what their subconscious is telling them they need and like. They can sense better what their body needs. But as an adult, that goes out of the window, and you eat what you are told to eat, or what the magazines tell you to eat, which right now is all the green juices, or avocado on toast. Or you go the other way and indulge every taste you like, regardless of what your body is telling you you need, such as pizzas and sweets. In my case, I have always swung wildly between the two, either bingeing on McDonald's, Chinese, Domino's and chocolate when I didn't feel worthy of eating healthily – or eating insanely healthily as I didn't feel I deserved the other stuff until I was as skinny as I could be.

So conscious eating is like trying to see your food the way that a child does, where you eat what you need in moderation and trust what your body tells you. I have been trying to do this since last summer, and I swear it has turned my whole world on its head – in a good way!

It makes so much sense. If you sense that you smell, you shower. If you sense that your body needs something, you should eat it. Most people do this when they are ill and trying to recover. Like what do I need? Tomato soup, or dried toast, OK, have it. So it is about transferring this to everyday life. Why shouldn't you always trust your body's urges?

Once I learnt about this, it was a total game changer. Now when I wake up in the morning, I ask myself, 'What do I fancy? What is my body needing?' Some days it is porridge, others, it might be a bacon sandwich. But the aim is to trust the answer you get, and go with that.

I can often tell what frame of mind I am in by what I choose. If I go to Pret and my hand automatically goes for the salad that I really hate but is the one with the least calories, I know my eating disorder voice is trying to break through. Because normal happy well Grace would definitely choose something like the tuna sandwich or cheese toastie! It is amazing how many voices there are in your own head when it comes to food, and it is about realising which each of them are and focusing on the right ones, or at least balancing them out.

It is also about drowning out the external voices. Those that use terms such as 'cheat day' 'guilt-free food' and 'treats'. It is all bollocks. It just reiterates the guilt and shame around our diet, and when we are in a society with access to so many wonderful foods, having a happy and positive relationship with all those options is the way to be.

If you are like me, it won't be easy in the beginning. We are trained to eat what we are told to, or we have voices that have a stronger influence than they should. But I promise you, conscious eating is life-changing. If you don't already do it, try it!

Help with Eating Disorders

- **BEAT:** Beating eating disorders. Online advice, a search service for local advice, and chatrooms at www.beat.org or call 0345 634 1414 if you are an adult, or 0345 634 7650 for the youth line.

- **The Recover Clinic:** A London- and Brighton-based clinic that deals with eating disorders. Their website is www.therecoverclinic.co.uk. It is not cheap, I will warn you of that! But the treatment is amazing. You can start to dip your toe in to what the clinic is about by trying their app 'Recover & Me' which has videos about each area of recovery, medication and tasks to educate and empower.

Chapter 13
IF YOU DON'T LOOK AFTER YOURSELF, NO ONE ELSE WILL!

'Self-love is the number one ingredient.'

By 2016, everything was starting to go a bit nuts. TV was taking off with the various documentary talks and discussions with different channels, followed by filming with the BBC, then getting my own series on MTV, *The Truth About Sex With Grace Victory*. I was being asked to appear at all sorts of conferences and give talks at events and appear on panels with other women who I had great admiration for. I have always loved chatting with my followers online, but this was like taking it out to actually meet them in person. Not to mention that I was getting recognised out and about a lot too! I loved it when people came over for a quick chat and a photograph, but other times I would end up in deep conversations with people. Several times

I was late for meetings when a girl would stop me in the street to tell me their problems, and become tearful as they looked for advice. There was no way I wasn't going to stop and sit with them and formulate some kind of plan, give them some hope, before I headed on.

I took the idea that I was a role model very seriously, and was happy that I could make a difference to people's lives. It is a privilege that people allow me to step into their worlds for a bit, and that we get to know each other, and if I can sprinkle a bit of happiness on any shit they are going through, then that is perfect, job done!

But by summer 2016 I wasn't giving myself a minute off. If I wasn't at an event, or shoot, or filming, I was making videos, being interviewed, or helping people on social media. It was draining, and people began commenting on how tired and burnt out I was. Don't get me wrong, I was loving it and was so thankful for everything that was happening. When I first began working with my management in 2014 we put together a five-year plan, and it looked like we were well on our way to achieving it in half that time. But I have gone through enough problems with my mental health to know when I need to be taking more care of myself if I don't want it to spiral out of control, and I was beginning to hit one of those points.

Eventually the solution came when I learnt about self-care. This has become so crucial in my life now that I don't think I could ever do without it. Now I have set routines to look after myself, certain days when I don't work, or times when I step away from social media altogether. But I'm getting ahead of myself here. Let me explain it to you first!

SELF-CARE

Any activity you do voluntarily to help you maintain physical, mental and emotional health and wellbeing.

Most people are so busy getting their university work done, their to-do lists finished, or their latest project for work completed that they forget about looking after themselves. I don't mean as in forget to get dressed or put on make-up, I mean really look after the mental and physical side of their wellbeing.

It was something I had been failing to do as I was so focused on everything I needed to do for work and helping out people via my vlog that I had forgotten to take care of the person who I need to look after the most – myself. Once I could see that, I changed my whole outlook.

Self-care covers all sorts of actions and decisions that basically make you feel good about yourself. A lot of the time it is just small little things that make you happy, so it might be taking a long bath, burning your favourite candles, going for a walk, or just simply learning to take time out and say no to people, so you can enjoy an evening in your own company.

Seven Little Things that Make Me Happy

- Burning candles and incense. I love Jo Malone candles, lots of tea lights, and lots of £2 packs of incense that you can buy on Ebay. The flickering flames are hypnotic, and give that real sense of warmth and comfort to the room. Good smells are important as they can really make you relax and chill out. I also burn sticks of sage to get rid of negative energies and as the smell is so therapeutic. It makes my flat instantly nicer.

- Meditating. I try and take ten minutes out every day and meditate. Not like legs crossed and finger and thumbs circled, but just phone off, sitting in silence and trying to clear my mind of all thoughts. Deep breaths, and just being. I am always doing something or my mind is going a hundred miles an hour with thoughts, so the step away to slow down is very important. I believe it improves my thoughts the rest of the time and helps me sleep.

- Baking cookies. There is something so therapeutic about the process of baking. Alone in the kitchen with my thoughts, music on, following simple instructions, and perfect cookies at the end. Oh and they must include Nutella, as Nutella fixes everything!

- Googling 'cute dogs'. If you have never done this, I swear it will change your life – or your mood at least!*

- Putting on freshly washed PJs. That is literally up there with the most amazing things ever in life. An instant mood boost.

- Dancing to a great song. Putting on a ridiculous old song like 50 Cent's 'Candy Shop', then dancing round your lounge alone or with friends, is hard to beat!

- Buy new shoes. Because, well, really? You need me to explain this one?

Sounds easy, right? But almost all of us feel guilty taking a step back from everything else that needs done in life, and indulging

---

* N.B. no matter how much you like these dogs though, you are NOT to go and order one for delivery elsewhere on the internet. No matter how adorable they look, YOU MUST NOT! If you aren't sure why, watch my BBC3 documentary *The Cost of Cute: The Dark Side of the Puppy Trade* then come back to me …

in something that we need ourselves. Society seems to think if you dare to prioritise time for yourself, you are selfish or spoilt, but that is not the truth of it. Self-care should be an important part of each human's life. We all need to be kinder to ourselves, especially in this hectic, messed-up world that we seem to be living in right now, where everyone seems to be a bit anxious or depressed!

We also need to kick back on bosses who take advantage of the culture of 'work, work, work', where you are supposed to give every second of the day and night to them, then hold out till the weekend when, if you are lucky, you might get two days off to tick off everything else in your life's 'to-do' list. Forget that. If you need a break from work, take some holiday time. If you are sick, stop stressing you should be in the office, but have some time off to recover. Look after yourself. The fact you haven't is probably why you are ill and stressed in the first place.

Not that working for yourself is much easier. If, like me, you are ambitious and a very demanding boss to yourself, turning off and finding 'non-work' time can be equally hard, if not more so! It doesn't help that I love a list. In fact, my lists have sub-lists! And my mentality is always that I have to do one more job or task, and then that leads to another few that should also be done, and then oh look, I have pulled an all-nighter working on things, but I can't really afford to have much sleep as I need to be up the next day and on with other bits . . . THAT IS NOT SELF-CARE!!!!

For me now though, self-care is part of my daily routine. I wake up and play meditation music, and burn sage or incense, in order to start my day in a calm environment. Then on an average day I might do something small like preparing my favourite meal, or getting my nails done. I am also big on positive affirmations. I love a good saying, as anyone who follows any of my social media or videos will know. They can really sum up a feeling or situation in one perfectly formed line. But I also think it can be a helpful thing to have a list of positive affirmations that you say to yourself each day. Say something enough, and it will filter into your brain and you will believe it.

Positive Affirmations

These are the ones I repeat to myself every morning, but everyone should find their own phrases that work for them, so only use these as a starting point:

- 'I am good enough, I am worthy of love, I deserve to be happy.'
- 'I have the courage to stand firm-footed in the ground and bounce back after knockbacks.'
- 'My thoughts become things. Whatever I think, I shall be.'
- 'Everything I'm not, makes me everything I am.'

Other days, if I have been going through a tricky time, I need more self-care. So I might allocate a full day to looking after myself and getting myself back on track. Maybe it seems indulgent, but if one day off makes for six productive days, is that not better than seven sluggish, half-arsed, miserable days? It is about care for me, provided by me, as though I have given myself one big hug.

Things to Do to Be Kind to Yourself

If you need a real mental step away from the rest of the world for a day, consider some of these options:

- Delete your social media apps. From time to time it is healthy to do this for a few days, or for as long as you need, so you don't waste time scrolling and comparing yourself to others.

- Clean or organise something. There is something very therapeutic about a good clear-out, whether it is your underwear drawer – where let's face it, you will find eight unworn bras you forgot you even owned – or your DVD collection, which I bet is filled with films you know deep down you will never watch again.

- Give back. If you can afford to, donate to a charity that rings true to you, or help someone in need.

- Give yourself a reason to celebrate. Perhaps you have passed an exam or finally cleared fuckboy out of your life. Whatever it is, celebrate!

- Appreciate. Write a list of all the things you are grateful for, and focus on those.

- Have a new experience. Go to a theme park, a spa, a circus . . . somewhere you have never been but want to. Whatever your heart desires!

The best way to work out how to self-care is to think of yourself as a little child, and how you would nurture that child to make them better. Think about your inner child, that person inside you, and what would make them happier and more content within themselves. It might sound daft to think about yourself in the third person, but for me it is the best way to look at it objectively, and not feel self-indulgent.

Or if you feel that is too much, think of yourself like your best friend. How would you help her if she needed a bit of a boost? Does she just need an evening of watching her favourite chick flicks and switching off from everything else? Would an evening with all social media disconnected be the best thing, so she can step back from being consumed by everything she is reading, and relax for a few hours? Or is she simply a bit sad and some candles and pampering will help her relax? Sometimes mental health issues can mean you view yourself in such a poor light that you really cannot see what you mentally or physically need. In those cases, having a doctor or therapist guide you on it can be a helpful thing.

Self-care is all about cleansing your mental state and taking time out just for you. It takes a while to get into the routine and habit of it, though, and you do have to work at it. It is difficult in the beginning as it can feel foreign to your body and mind, but once you start doing it and reaping the benefits, I promise you will be calmer, more relaxed, and it will become second nature!

Eight Things to Do on your Period

Ah, that time of the month. The five or so days out of every thirty that all girls dread, right? Nope, not me! If anything, I'd have to admit that I look forward to it . . . Yes, you heard me right. OK, so of course I feel bloated and extra fat, my back and boobs hurt, my stomach is cramping, my skin looks like death and don't get me started on the emotional rollercoaster.

But . . . it is also the time I remember I am a woman, that my period means I am capable – hopefully – of having children one day.

At ten years old, I already had B-cup boobs, a hairy vagina and hairy armpits. Then one day I went to the loo and there was a brown mark in my knickers. I hadn't had any cramps or pains, but I guessed what it was, and I shouted out: 'Mum! I think I've started my period!'

She brought me some sanitary towels in, and that was it. No dramas, no tears, no celebrations. I just knew it for what it was, accepted it, did what I needed to deal with it, and got on with it. I think that has been my relationship with my period ever since.

It's clearly not like that for everyone, though. My sister was hysterical, screaming and crying about the blood. I couldn't understand why. You are becoming a woman; you are ready to take on the world!

Even the monthly process of it I like. I know that sounds weird, but it is like the stresses of the whole month are coming out. It is the perfect excuse to just self-care to the max!

When I learnt about self-care I decided the best way to get through the painful bits of my period was to embrace them, to accept feeling crap, and use it as an excuse to spoil myself. It is every girl's chance to indulge herself and no one – yourself included – can make you feel guilty, as what better excuse do you have than Mother Nature is about to come and fuck your shit up?!

Over time my list of indulgences has grown and developed, and I really do look forward to wallowing in those five days of the month. Here is my current list – give me a shout if you have any suggestions to add to it, as I am always up for expanding on it!

1. Cry. You know you want to, so just go with it, unashamed big sobs if that is what you need. This is your chance to get out all the emotional shit that you have built up over the last month, and you have the perfect excuse. Plus you know how much better you will feel after all that weight has been lifted off your shoulders . . .

2. Eat more of your favourite food, and that obviously includes junk food, but don't see it as that. Remember all food is food, and in that respect it is all equal. Order your favourite takeaway – for me that is Chinese – but get curry, pizza, chips, whatever you're feeling, and enjoy the luxury of not cooking. Then of course round it off with chocolate. Science says chocolate encourages your body to release endorphins, which in turn make you happy, and you can't argue with science, right?

3. Spoil your body. Do whatever you need to make yourself physically unwind, and to let your body relax. For me that is no make-up on, hair in a top-knot, and a warm bath with candles and a really luxurious product. My current favourite is Jo Malone's shower oils, which are really intense and oily, and make your skin feel so much softer, and me feel much better.

4. Indulge in comforting habits, so whatever you wish you could do every single day but feel you can't, do it now. Watch

your favourite box sets back to back, curled on your sofa with a warm blanket and a strategically positioned hot water bottle – or several.

5. Make sure your clothes reflect that key word 'comfort' too. Tracksuits, leggings, oversized hoodies and trainers are my staple, and if I have to wear a bra, it must be super comfy – with sore nipples the last thing I need is a fancy lacy thing. If I must go outside, a denim jacket over the top at least makes it more stylish. If you have to be presentable in an office I'd scrap the idea of tight trousers and heels, but focus on loose-fitting floaty dresses with tights, that giant stretchy, airy product! But get those PJs and fluffy socks on as soon as you are home.

6. Wearing comfortable stuff doesn't mean you can't think ahead to nicer clothes, though. Retail therapy is a must at this time, though obviously only from the comfort of your sofa! Treat yourself to a new outfit online, so you can focus on how you will look and feel when you are less bloated and feel like you again. ASOS is my favourite website for this, and the next-day delivery option means you don't have to wait long.

7. If you have a boyfriend, this is your chance to moan at him about whatever you like. It doesn't matter how stupid it is, as he can't have a go back at you, when you are clearly in a vulnerable and sensitive state. In fact, he should make you feel better by going and getting you more chocolate. Right now.

8. If you want to go a step further in indulging yourself, check out one of the companies that has sprung up in the last few

years selling monthly care packages. A little box gets delivered to your door containing a mix of sanitary products and treats like teas, sweet stuff and beauty products. Go on, you know you deserve it.

Now what did I say about loving your periods? Have I convinced you yet? I bet you all can't wait for your next period now!

Chapter 14
IF YOU CAN'T HANDLE ME AT MY WORST, YOU DON'T DESERVE ME AT MY BEST

'Surround yourself with people that don't make you feel like you are hard to love.'

O ne of the key things that has helped me through many of the lows in my life has been friendship. I finally have a great bunch of females around me and I love them to bits. We have each other's backs, we are there for each other no matter what, and crucially, we are positive influences in each other's lives. They are my squad!

But finding them has not been easy and has taken a lot of mistakes. I had to work out what a friend is *not*, before I could realise what a friend *is*. In the process I have learnt that not all friendships are healthy, no matter how much fun that person may seem, and that the best thing to do is to walk away from a toxic friend before you get sucked in by their negativity. In other cases the friendships are great, but are not meant to last forever. Friendships can work for one period of your life, but not sustain themselves as you move on and change, and that is OK.

I have learnt that friendships are not about numbers, and it is better to have a few amazing, trustworthy friends who truly know and understand you, than a huge social network who don't have your back when it comes to the crunch.

I find it very easy to make friends, but harder to sustain them. I think in part that is because people are drawn to the extroverted part of my personality, but when they realise I don't always want to go out drinking and partying, and that I am an introvert on a lot of levels, they drift away. A lot of that, I think, is the industry I work in. But I need friends that are actual friends and can hang out with me, talk about deep and important things, and are happy relaxing and gossiping over take-out. Real organic, true, honest friendships are really important to me.

I have friends from back in High Wycombe who remind me where I am from and keep me grounded, so that I am still the same person I always was. We do the same shit we always did, like go to TGI Fridays and have cocktails and Jack Daniel's chicken wings. I'll never get tired of doing that!

The one I see most is Laren, who I have been friends with since I was twelve. She and her family have always been brilliant at showing the other side of my culture. She is black, and growing up they would listen to reggae music and cook amazing Caribbean food. It is a place for me to explore the other side of who I am. When we were younger we would go to dance-offs and just hang out, and at one point when I was particularly depressed I moved out of Mum's and in with them, and it gave me a fresh perspective and a pick-up. She doesn't look at me any differently now than she did then, and I love catching up with her.

I don't see many of those school friends I talked about – the ex-bullies, who on the whole were pretty fake. While so many teenagers see secondary school as their entire life, and think everything that happens there is *the* be all and end all, I somehow was always quite good at having a view of the bigger picture. I knew school wouldn't be my life forever, and life there wasn't how it would always be. Perhaps I was able to think like this because I had so much going on outside of school.

I'd love to still be close to my stage school pals, but things drifted after everyone headed off after college, and while we have some contact, they are scattered around the world in places like Abu Dhabi and New York, all on their amazing adventures.

Unfortunately, in recent years I have had my share of friendships that should never have happened. I didn't always realise it at first, but interestingly as I have become healthier and more confident, it's as though I have been able to see people for who they are. Sadly I discovered when you have mental health issues you can develop 'unwell relationships' that actually fuel your insecurities, rather than helping them.

I also had a problem with people who were only there for what I could give them through my job, whether that was access to free holidays, or a few more Twitter followers.

Even when I did begin to realise who the negative people in my life were, I didn't initially act on it, as I think I was scared of being lonely. I also thought I would have to replace that friend-ship and had no idea how to go about doing that. But as I became more confident in myself and saw just how draining these friendships were on me, I didn't hesitate in cutting them off. People think that is brutal, but I have been badly burnt, and you can't dwell on feeling bad about people who aren't good for you. The reality is you need to protect yourself, and if friends don't have your best intentions at heart, well, they aren't your friends. Now I listen to what I know in my heart about people without fail.

While these negative experiences aren't great to go through, I think for me they have added to me really finding out who I am, who I want to be, and who I want around me while I get there.

It is also very telling if once the friendship has ended you look back at it with hindsight and don't like what you see. Or if not one bit of you actually misses the friendship and there is no hole where you imagined there would be.

It is good to look at a person as an outsider. Would I want to see my other friends hanging out with them? If I had a daughter, would I want them to be friends?

Despite all my tough talk about moving on though, I still find it really difficult to go through the end of a friendship. Perhaps it is the knowledge of the time I have wasted on the person that hurts more than anything. The loyalty, positivity, honesty I had given them, when I wasn't getting that in return.

I have learnt that it is better to be alone than with people who aren't great for you, so you should never tolerate a bad friend-ship. Also friendships don't have to be replaced; you just look out for healthier ones.

Clues to a Toxic Friendship

As women I do believe we know deep down if the vibe we are getting off a person is a sign of a good or toxic friendship. So rule number one is if you are not feeling it, trust yourself. A few other obvious signs of a toxic friend for me are:

- A friend who never asks how you are. If they text you all their great news, or look for support through their shit times, but never once check in with how you are feeling, they are just plain selfish and a bad friend with no interest in you.

- If someone is constantly cussing or bashing other people they hang around with, you have to question what they could be saying about you behind your back. Two-faced behaviour is not an attractive friendship quality.

- Friends that only want to be around you through the bad times, who increase their own self-worth by seeing you worse off, sadder or more depressed than them. No one needs that negativity!

- Inversely friends that only want to be around you for the good times. So people who want to party with you, latch on to your success, and practically claim your success for themselves. If a friend is suddenly nowhere to be seen as soon as things get difficult, you don't need that person in your life!

The advantage of going through a really bad period with friends and being forced to re-evaluate who and what matters, is that it then becomes clearer who the good friends are, and you really appreciate them.

I have a really good, close set of friends right now, and I want to namecheck them here and now! They have really shown me what friendship is.

Stand up Danie and Chloe in particular, as well as my gorgeous spiritual sisters in the States.

They all tell me how it is, lift me up when I am down, make me see things when they aren't really clear to me, make me laugh, have my back . . . all the qualities that really matter in a true friend. It is nice to have friends I can actually lean on in difficult situations, which is not something I have ever done in the past. I have never trusted people enough, or believed that they were capable of supporting me without me losing some independence and owing them something. But with these girls, it is without an agenda; support is given with no expectation, just purely because they care.

Chloe in particular has been a huge influence on me in changing my views and my life! I am not sure I will ever repay her for helping me not just day to day, but being a true friend through difficult situations, particularly in 2016, and days I am not even sure I can make it. I hope that I give at least some of that back to them all though too, as I do think it is important for friendships to be two-way streets.

I met them all through the internet, through blogging and Twitter, which is ironic, as I am forever telling people to get off the internet and go and make real friends, then it is like, 'Oh shit, that is where I have made my best ones . . .!' But you never know where your friends will pop up from; you just need to embrace them once you have got them.

A Good Friend Will . . .

- . . . Support you no matter what. Even if they don't believe in the decisions you are making, they will try to understand why you are making them.

- . . . At the same time, tell you about yourself if you are being a bitch. They will tell you the truth, even if it is going to hurt you, if it will ultimately help you to know it.

- . . . Care that you succeed, get the career you want and earn good money, but they will also realise that success in this area is just an element of you, it is not all of you.

- . . . Hang at your house and be equally happy chatting or sitting in relaxed silence, while you munch on take-out. They see you with no make-up, looking your worst, but you don't have to try to be something you are not or put on pretences.

- . . . Have good intentions towards you, and you will know right deep down in your gut that you can trust them. When they see you, there is no agenda other than to spend time with a person they like.

- . . . Value your friendship, and understand and respect what the friendship means to you as well as what it means to them.

- . . . See you regularly, and not just on social media! But if something happens that keeps you apart – if one of you goes travelling or is tied up on a huge project – when you see each other again you go straight back into your usual friend mode, and can relax with them as though you saw them just the day before.

Quotes from my Squad on Friendship

I asked my closest friends to give me their definition of true friendship. I figured as they are all so good at it, they should know! So here are their pearls of wisdom. Enjoy ☺

Vix: 'Friendship doesn't mean "always being there". People have their own lives and own paths. You don't have to speak to someone every five minutes to be a good friend. However, friendship does mean being there when you are needed. Knowing your friend needs something before they have to ask. And if they do ever have to ask, they know you will be there for them.'

Laren: 'No matter how much time you are apart, or the distance you live from each other, you are always there for one another, just a phone call away.'

Lottie: 'I love the kind of friendship where you could stop talking to each other for weeks because you're both just out there living your lives but when you catch up it's nothing but love and being excited to hear about what your friend has been up to. I love hearing what Gracie's been up to because it is always either a) inspiring as hell, or b) mad as hell, and either way I just love hearing about it! That's what friendship is to me, sharing your life with your squad, cheering each other on, and calling each other out when you need to. Real friends have your back no matter what, and that's what I have with Grace.'

Steph: 'The definition of friendship has always been an iffy one for me. I never understood its meaning until I met my best friend as a teenager and from there built a squad around me of beautiful and strong women. I'm proud to say I cherish the girls in my life that define friendship.'

Callie: 'Friendship is about growth, change and understanding, and being friends with Grace in such a short time has created a wonderful growth in myself and also her. When I first met Grace for a photoshoot on a major magazine we clicked because we were from such similar backgrounds. She was the confident, independent, powerful woman she still is now, but beneath the surface I knew she struggled with her body image. And whilst I was at a point of full confidence in my body, I lacked full confidence in myself and my personal career goals. Together a friendship formed and over time (amongst the many laughs, many tears, and many shared bags of crisps) we helped build each other up, motivate each other to see the best in ourselves, to learn to believe that we deserved happiness regardless of whether we fitted the typical beauty standard. I'm grateful for Grace always pushing me to work harder, be better, and accept that what is meant for me will not pass me by.'

Akua: 'You know when you have created a friendship, it is like a spark goes off between two people and a decision is made. The test of true friendship is similar to what they say the test of true love is. Allowing that person to drift away from you. Friendship knows no space and time.'

Erica: 'I've had more than my fair share of "friends" but the real ones make you understand what it truly means to be unconditionally loved and accepted. They encourage, uplift and inspire, with no strings attached. You may not see them for months at a time, but as soon as you speak it's as if no time has passed. They understand you almost instantly upon meeting you and you just know that when things get rough you will always be there (with donuts and pizza) and they will too.'

Nai Nai: 'They say you are what you attract, and if that is true my friends are the biggest compliment the universe could have ever given me. They are nothing short of wonderful. Friends show you both who you are and what you can be. It is through those relationships you can live in both the present and the future at the same time.'

Danielle: 'Grace, you are the definition of a "girl boss". You push me to be a better person and my life is fuller now you are by my side. I feel at ease in your company, so, so comfortable, and I can't get over how much we laugh when we are together. Friendship means the world to me and I couldn't be prouder of the things you've achieved. Go get it, Grace, you deserve the world. Xx'

Chloe: 'Friendship to me is centred around trust and loyalty. I love having people I can tell anything to, and them me – we don't judge each other, we are just honest. They are your wee support system tribe, with you through good and bad. If you find a keeper look after them, fight for them, respect them and nurture your relationship with them, because they are truly invaluable.'

Chapter 15
LOVE IS NEVER LIKE THE MOVIES

'The truth is, everyone is going to hurt you. You've
just got to find the ones worth suffering for.'
Bob Marley

I love a romantic film. The perfect couple, destined to be
together from the off, but having to go through all sorts of
trials and tribulations to get there, until they reach their
lovely happy ending where they live happily ever after. Well, real
life isn't bloody well like that, is it?! Hell no, us actual real-life
people have to go through heartache, disappointment, time
invested in fuckboys who mess with our heads, and sometimes
even humiliation.

I kinda knew love wasn't really like the movies from the start,
though. Think about everything I saw growing up – it was more
like an advert for the anti-Hollywood version! But there is probably a secret bit of everyone who hopes for that perfect love
story regardless.

When I was thirteen, I thought I had found it with Aaron, in that innocent way you believe in your first love. Then of course he was my first experience of a break-up, when I thought the world was going to end.

But as everyone always finds out, that first cut isn't necessarily the deepest, but it is one that hurts because it is such a shock. It doesn't become less painful with time, but you become slightly more adept at dealing with it and learn how to bounce back.

I have noticed that with each heartbreak, there seems to be a definite pattern to my thought process and the healing methods I go through. It doesn't actually seem to matter if it is the guy or me who does the breaking up, the same things happen. There are four definite stages and I think a lot of people – female at least – go through the same ones.

Stage one: I am absolutely distraught and blame myself. I analyse every little detail of the relationship, and go through all sorts of emotional ups and downs. I am completely wrapped up in the pain, hurt and confusion, and need to be alone with my thoughts. I know a lot of people need their mates at this stage, but for me they come later on. When things get difficult, I like to deal with the shit by myself first.

Stage two: The shame and embarrassment kicks in too. What if someone asks if I am still with him? Then I have to admit I am not, we broke up. Then they might pity me, or discuss me with other people, or I'll not be able to answer without crying.

Stage three: After a few weeks the depressive clouds clear a bit, but then the anger kicks in. Suddenly my thoughts are more along the lines of: how dare he? I am a great person. Around this time I will start seeing my friends again, as now I am stronger. They can listen to my rants, and add their own encouragement into the mix. I don't want to be alone in case my head does start to go off on a negative spiral again, but my friends can talk me out of that.

Stage four: Once the anger is out of my system, I start to feel better. I get a lot of clarity and things start to fall back into perspective. I feel more adult about everything and don't think about the break-up or my ex every minute of the day. Normal life begins to resume again.

That is me anyhow, and talking to friends, it seems to be a pretty similar cycle for most girls. Weirdly I think it has also helped for me to recognise the process, in terms of getting through it. I've gone through a break-up before where, because I have almost known my routine, I told myself right from the start: 'Right, you have a week to cry, and that is it. You can cry solid tears 24/7 if you want but that is definitely the maximum. Then you will move on to the next stage.' Then it was a case of allowing myself on to the shame, then the anger, then making sure I moved on from that back to real life.

You have to remember that if someone has hurt you, it is healthy to acknowledge what has happened and allow yourself to feel that hurt, but there is also a balance. If you stick in phases one to three for too long it becomes a question of: is that person still hurting you now, or are you hurting yourself? If the honest answer is the latter one, then you are getting stuck in a hole, and it is time to spread your wings and get back on with life. Remember my earlier chapter 'Stop Wallowing in Self-Pity'? Well that applies here!

I do think generally women feel the break-up the deepest in the weeks straight after, but then perhaps fall into a more practical mind-set after a bit. Whereas for whatever reason, it is different with men, and they often seem to act like they don't give a shit straight after a break-up. They are out with their friends, acting all cool, loving life. Then a few weeks or months down the line, it hits them. They realise what they no longer have and then panic. Without fail every boyfriend I have split up with has come back to see if we can rekindle things. Obviously they realise how great I am and want me back!

My most recent break-up was in 2016, and this time I added my self-care routines into the week I was alone in the immediate aftermath. I think it really helped get me on the road to recovery. Yes, I was crying, but at least I was crying in a warm bath with a bar of chocolate in my hand!

Like I always say, you can never grow if you are comfortable, you have to go through some kind of shit. So, horrible though heartbreak is, like so much else in life, you really do learn from it and come out the other side a stronger person.

Once I am at stage four and out of the heartbreak I do look back and think, 'Wow, that was pretty dramatic, but you have survived it, everything is fine, and life goes on, don't you know?' But you have no power to see that until you have got there. That knowledge only comes with hindsight. In the midst of it you need to follow where your emotions need to go. But afterwards, you can actually learn from it. I've looked back and realised I've been a total bitch in the relationship, and it is no wonder the guy wanted to leave. There was a time in my life I can honestly say I wasn't very good to boyfriends. I would lie a lot and be horrible, because of issues I was going through that were nothing to do with them. The poor guys would take the full force of my stress whenever any of it came bursting out, but then it would come back and bite me on the arse when I suddenly found myself alone.

We all make mistakes though and all you can do is think, 'Right, I fucked up. Lesson learnt.' It is so difficult, I know, but you come out the other end that bit more resilient.

As a result I am a lot more honest with my boyfriends now. I will talk about my feelings and as I've got older I've become more compassionate towards them, and what they are going through.

You just need to make sure you choose the right kind of guys, and don't go for fuckboys. Lord, I have dated my share of them, and it is all well and good working on yourself to become a good girlfriend, but if you choose the wrong guy, well, you are setting yourself up for a fall . . .

Signs You Are Dating a Fuckboy

Argh, fuckboys. We all get attracted to them and sucked into their bullshit at some point, don't we? Come on, agree with me, I don't want to feel like I am on my own here! Putting this list together has really irritated me though, as yes, I have experienced every single thing on this list. How can I have put up with such crap?

But you know what? Now I know the signs, I can see a fuckboy coming a mile off, and I ain't never going near one again! Please take note, and run away at the first sign of any of the below . . .

1. He is disrespectful to his mum. If a man (#boy) can't treat his mum with respect, there is absolutely no way in hell he is

ever going to treat you – or anyone else – with respect either, no matter how much he might be pretending to right now.

2. He has no ambition. If a guy is in a dead-end job – or no job at all – and completely happy with the situation, I've got to question that. Someone who doesn't ever want to strive to be better is not for me.

3. He constantly cancels on you. This is my biggest pet peeve. I was in a situation a few years ago where I was dating a guy and he would always cancel on me. And not like the day before, but TEN MINUTES before he was to pick me up. Make-up on, dating mind in place, thoughts wondering to whether I was going to have sex . . . then I'd get let down. A boy like this is a timewaster; move on.

4. He always asks for nude photos. This is wrong on so many levels. First of all, the amount of trust I would need to have in a guy to keep them just to himself is like, we would need to be *married* or something. Sending photos is really dangerous and you leave yourself so vulnerable. Besides, why do you need the photo when you see me naked when we have sex? Or if we haven't even reached that stage, even worse; why do you think I would give you that access?! I think it is something that no girl should ever do. It is not worth the risk, so for me the answer will always be no. Just no.

5. He always ignores your text messages and calls. A fuckboy loves to leave you hanging, and mostly gets round to responding only when he wants something. On the other hand, if you don't answer his calls or reply to his texts in seconds, then all hell breaks loose. Avoid.

6. He never wants to go on dates with you. If a guy doesn't want to be seen in public with you, you have to ask why. The truth is you are basically one big giant secret, his

friends don't even know who you are. Maybe he's calling you 'just some girl' or 'a ting'. Yup, been there. Being taken on dates and publicly acknowledged is a thing I feel very strongly about.

7. He slut shames. He tells you a story about a girl he calls a slut and describes something she did with him. This is wrong on two levels. I have been sat there before thinking, 'What? I do that on a regular basis, oh God!' but having to pretend all like, 'Oh, really? How bad!' while dying inside. But on another level my mind is going, 'But wait, *you* did that with the girl, yet *you* are getting on a moral high ground about it! Like, were you *forced* into participating or something?' Hypocrite.

8. He parties without you and you only know from social media. If *for example* you think he is having a night in, then he puts a photo up on Facebook of him holding a bottle of Cîroc in a club. A club you know a lot of his female friends hang out in. Definitely a fuckboy and time to end it.

9. He never asks if you are OK. This basically means he doesn't give a shit about your welfare, but just cares how clean your pussy is. Harsh but true. If you keeled over tomorrow he wouldn't really care, so get out of there while you can!

I wasn't going to talk about Simon in this book as our relationship is a very private thing to me, but also hugely precious, and I worry about putting it out there in the limelight to be inspected and judged and commented on. But at the same time I am trying to be completely honest with you guys, and talk about the important bits in my life, and well, he has been and still is a hugely important part of my journey and my life.

Besides, if he reads this and he isn't in it, he might get offended, haha!

I met Simon at an R&B gig years ago. I knew the singer through YouTube who was performing that night, and Simon was his drummer so we got talking. It was another eighteen months after that, though, in July 2014, that we actually got together.

Once that had happened, things moved very quickly. We went to New York together after we had been dating for just three months, and when I left Mum's home and moved to London to get my own flat in February 2015, he moved in with me.

People were surprised, as on paper, you wouldn't put us together. There is me: mixed-race, from a council estate, and into my R&B, and there is him: white, posh – or middle-class at the very least (come on, he had a nanny when he was little, lol) – and into rock music. But for whatever reason there was chemistry, we clicked, and it worked. We had so much fun together, and his sense of humour was dry and clever, and I just felt positive and as though life was great when he was there.

I had fallen for him in a big way, and as I was so proud to be with him, I happily talked about him in my videos. He appeared in a lot of the day-to-day ones within weeks of us getting together, and people got to see his fun, thoughtful and chilled-out side. We also made a few together where we talked about important issues, such as 'What Boys Really Think of us Naked – Q&A with my Boyfriend' where poor Simon was so careful to say exactly the right thing, both to keep me happy, but also to be responsible in the message he was giving those who were watching.

Things between us were really passionate, but also turbulent and we rowed a fair bit. It was the first time I had lived away from my mum, and I was getting used to the independence and responsibility of that, as well as throwing every possible hour into my career. At the same time Simon was the first boyfriend I had lived with, so I had a lot of learning to do on that front, and it proved to be a lot in one go. I found it difficult trying to care for him and put time into us, as well as myself.

But then a load of things in a row got on top of me. I started putting weight back on and struggled with that, and then I had the horrific Twitter falling-out with my best friend. Then this might sound weird, but Demi Lovato released a song called 'Father' and it felt like it opened up wounds I had been ignoring.

It was a gorgeous song about her conflicted emotions over the father that had left her family when she was two. I would listen to it over and over, and became quite focused on everything that had happened with my dad. The emotions I had suppressed for so long about him abandoning us came to the surface. I began thinking about all the important people in my life who had left me, from both family and friends, and I decided that as I loved Simon so much, it meant there was no way he was going to stay with me. That was just the way of the world, at least for me.

Ironically, Simon seemed to be the first guy I had dated who didn't come with a whole host of his own problems. He hadn't had a load of trauma in his own life, and wasn't dealing with his own issues. In fact he was – and is – pretty stable!

Maybe subconsciously I didn't think I was good enough to be with someone who cared about me. He respected me, which was amazing, which perhaps came from growing up with a mum and sister who he is close to, and who are influential on his life.

Also – and this might sound bizarre, so stick with me! – I am not sure I knew how to love him. No one had ever really shown me what a properly functioning, loving relationship looked like. Mum and Dad obviously didn't give me a demonstration of it, and nor did any of the other men in my family. Plus none of my previous relationships had been particularly healthy or an ideal example of how love should be.

As a result, I kept pushing Simon away and being horrible to him, already resenting him for the break-up which I was so sure would come. Unsurprisingly in March 2016 he then did decide he had had enough, and things were over between us. Of course when it happened it was horrific and felt like yet another low blow at a point in my life when I wasn't in a position to deal with it. But at the same time it was like he proved me right in my fears – here I was, being abandoned by another man, just as I suspected would happen. Even if I didn't realise I had been the catalyst for the whole thing!

Four months after we split, a couple we both knew were going through a really difficult time, and as part of helping them, Simon and I started talking again. It was initially very difficult as I was very angry with him for leaving me, but he got me to understand just how much I had pushed him away. It was quite a wake-up call for me, and flagged up how I had been repeating patterns I had learnt previously.

We started dating again, but it was too soon. By then I had finished filming for *Clean Eating's Dirty Secrets*, and was in the middle of counselling with Emmy. So the painful memories that had been starting to bubble up were combined with others that she encouraged me to revisit, and I was completely wrapped up with that and struggling to cope. I was unbearable to be around, and Simon realised I clearly wasn't ready to be back in a relationship.

I was mad, as I felt he had left me at a time when I needed him the most. I had needed support as I relived the trauma through counselling, but he had found it too hard. He explained to me my mental health problems had been really impacting on him, and that he had needed to step away for his own sanity. There is only so much a person can take, I guess, even from a person they love.

But as 2016 went on, I was learning coping mechanisms, and memories that had been causing me problems became properly dealt with and filed away – not to hide from but just as something that was in the past.

Simon and I carried on talking and in November we decided to get back together properly. Now I see it that we needed that time apart to learn more about ourselves – or I'm not sure about Simon, but I certainly did! In hindsight, I can see that I was going through so much emotionally and mentally that I needed to work on me before I could be in a relationship and give part of myself to someone else as well.

It took us a lot of time, and talking, to find the right balance again in our relationship, but this time around it feels a lot healthier. We have worked out our compromises and have practically stopped arguing. We also communicate a lot more, and are sure that while we are there for each other, we also give each other space when we need to. Simon has shown me that although he is a guy, he does still have insecurities, and worries about silly things as well. At the same time he reassures me that all the things I worry about are so meaningless to him. He is with me for me, and something like my inverted nipples or stretch-marks are not going to change that! We hang out together and do lots of things as a couple, but we also need that time on our own. It is like a whole new relationship and it is amazing.

This time though we decided to keep our relationship private to start with, and decided to just let friends and family know – kind of like normal people away from the vlogging world. We had learnt our lesson, and it had made it much harder when we had first split to have it analysed and discussed on the internet.

I didn't tell my followers we were back together for a good few months, as I kind of felt I would jinx things. But at the same time I always like to be honest with my followers so felt a bit strange about it, so once I was confident that me and Simon were really back on track, I began mentioning him again in my life updates. I didn't want to make our relationship as big a deal this time though, so decided we wouldn't make any videos together.

Simon is one of the best things that has ever happened to me. He has never tried to change me, but has loved me when I was at my biggest, and when I was at my thinnest. He has always accepted me for who I am and supported me in any way he can. If I am stressed he gives me a massage, if I am being a bitch he will tell me, and if I am stressed after therapy he will cook me dinner and listen to me talk. In return, I encourage him as he pushes ahead on his dreams, especially his music career. He describes me as his rock, and of course I help him look good by choosing his clothes! It is all the simple things in life that make a person happy. The little things that no one has ever done for me before and that I enjoy doing for someone else. I do want to get married and have children one day, and the way things are right now, I hope that will be with Simon. We just make a perfect little team.

Of course it is not all like the movies. It is not happy all the time, and even in the best relationships in the world, you do go through some shit, but Simon has never given up on me. Even when we had split he would still check in with mutual friends to see how I was doing, and he tells me he hoped that at some point I would get through my issues and we would be able to give it another go. I am glad I was able to fulfil that. It is hard to explain what our love is like, but we get it and understand it, and that is what matters.

The more I have learnt to believe in myself, I have accepted that it is possible for me to be loved by someone as amazing as Simon. As I have learnt to love myself, I have come to realise that I do deserve to be with someone who thinks of me as if I am magic, and it is great, because it really has that positive effect on me – sometimes I believe I am a little bit magic now too!

P.S. If I needed just one reason to stay with him, he makes fajitas to die for . . .

Chapter 16
DEAR FAMILY

'We came from battered and broken roots, but the sun will shine again and we'll blossom.'
Charlotte Victory

Since the time I told my dad to get out of the house when I was fifteen years old I have only seen him a handful of times. Once he turned up at the house where we were spending Christmas, with no warning, just arrived on the doorstep. But someone told him we weren't there and he went away. I don't know what had made him hunt us out that particular day. Maybe he was having a moment of sentimentality, or more than likely he had nowhere else to go and was feeling sorry for himself, but I was annoyed that he thought he could just turn up like that, and everything would be fine.

Other times I have bumped into him in High Wycombe when I was least expecting it, so on a bus when I had to do a double-take as he had gone grey, or walking out of a nail salon, in my own world and unprepared for it. Each time we exchanged four or five words, but it was awkward and I'd say we were both keen to get out of there. There is nothing I want to say to him really. Well, actually there is lots I want to say to him, but it is not anything that he will listen to.

Did you actually want me?

Why couldn't you have been there for us growing up?

How did you think your treatment of Mum was ever OK?

If you could do it all over again, would you be any different?

I know they say you can't miss what you never had, but I don't think that is true with him. There is a big space in my life where he should have been. I think a lot of the time my anger is directed at what he is not, rather than what he is, at all the things I wish he had been, but that he failed to be. I am angry he wasn't there, that he wasn't a role model to me, that he wasn't a good partner to my mum, or a father to me and Charlotte.

The reality is he is a coward, a waste of space, a dickhead who has never taken responsibility for his actions. The fact that he is my dad makes me ashamed of him.

I don't even really know him, and he doesn't know me. I couldn't tell you any basic facts about him, like what his favourite colour is, what take-out he would order, or if he has a favourite jumper he refuses to get rid of.

He doesn't know where I have been on holiday, who my best friends are, or what my GCSE results were. Just basic stuff that I could tell you about so many other people.

All I really know is the bits I hear through the family grapevine. So I knew that for a while he was in and out of security jobs. Then bizarrely I heard recently that he is the childminder for my uncle's son, a role I cannot imagine him taking on unless he has hugely changed as a person and grown up. But if he has, wouldn't he ever think he should get in touch with Charlotte and me, and try to make amends in some way? Maybe he knows it is too late, because I do think it is. I'm not sure I could really forgive him for everything that has come before. He has had twenty-six years to come good; I think that is more than enough time for anyone.

When I was about ten, I discovered that I had two older half-sisters through Dad, called Karlene and Sharina. They lived over in Slough and I was excited to meet up with them. I liked the idea of having older sisters at first, but then it became clear they didn't want to make the effort to get to know us, and our relationship didn't develop. There was also tension between us as we got older too, as I would feel resentful when I heard about Dad doing anything for them or helping them out, when he wasn't doing the same for us. They would make out that he was amazing, and I was like, 'Hell, no!'

I don't know if Dad is proud of my success, or what he even knows about it. I don't know if he has ever read any of my blogs, watched any of my videos, or made a point to catch one of my documentaries. There was one YouTube video in particular that I would obviously have loved him to watch. It was called 'Dear Dad' and it was very difficult to make, but felt like something I had to get out there. It only scraped the surface of my feelings for him as there is only so much you can put in a vlog, but a part of me really hoped he would see it. I have no idea if he has, but the sad reality is, knowing the kind of person he is, it wouldn't get through to him anyway. He wouldn't take responsibility, but would be pissed off at the accusations, and find ways to say, 'But it wasn't my fault!'

I feel real anger and disappointment when I think of him, but also sadness. I have tried to stop myself hating him, as I don't want to carry hatred of my father around with me for life, but I can't forgive him, nor can I forget him, so it is hard.

As for my mum, it is so hard to put into words my thoughts about her. On so many levels she is an absolute star who fought tooth and nail to give Charlotte and me the best childhood she knew how to. She had to take on the role of mum and dad, and even when Dad made her feel worthless and alone, she had to pull herself together and make life work for the sake of us all, the Three Musketeers.

I worry sometimes that she has never had a chance to be truly happy. She is so busy having to hold everything together for other people that she never really gets any time for herself, to focus on actually living for herself. I am sure if I told her to take some time out for self-care she would laugh at me, as though to say, 'Who has time for that?' But she is exactly the sort of person who deserves to step back from the stresses of everyday life for a few hours and really look after herself.

Mum is such a strong person, but she is also very damaged by the life she has lived. She has never gone into it in detail with me, but I know her dad physically abused her, so when she met my dad, it was like the cycle repeating itself for her. It worries me that she had no sense of self-worth growing up, and that is why she allowed someone like my dad into her life.

For a long time it terrified me that I would do the same thing: that although I hated what I have seen growing up, I would follow my parents' mistakes and end up repeating what they did, in the way that so many other people seem to do.

Because – and not to be unkind – Mum was a role model to me on lots of levels, but she was also an anti-role model. So she has shown me traits that I want to emulate, such as fighting for my children as she did for us. I want to be kind to them like her, and get them to talk to me openly about everything from school-work to sex. Mum is like a sister as well as my mum, and I want to be the same with my children.

But on the flip side she has shown me what I don't want to be. I will never repeat her mistakes in choosing a man who abuses me, or treats me like a second-class citizen. I will never give up my career and independence or give him money that I am sure is going on drugs. I will make sure that my own self-respect never slips and that I never lose sight of myself in the grips of an abusive man.

Mum's belief in me has seen me through some of my darkest times, and without her I would not be the person I am today. She still lives in the house in High Wycombe with Charlotte. I have a love-hate relationship with the town, which holds both great and awful memories for me. I will always have a soft spot for it, but I was also glad to leave it and much of its negativity behind. But I still wish I went back more often to see Mum and let her know how special she is.

I asked her if she wanted to say anything in the book. She has been the single most important person in my life, and it felt only right that she have her say! So she sent me this letter to include. Just the first line sent me into floods of tears.

Dear Grace,

I just wanted to let you know how proud I am of you and what you have achieved over the years. You work really hard, you're ambitious but you stay level-headed and remember where you came from. For you, your childhood was a struggle but you got through it and it has made you the strong woman you are today. We laughed, cried and had our ups and downs but I have never been disappointed in you, maybe a bit frustrated but never disappointed. For example, when you were younger and you really wanted to play outside, just before a school performance. Subsequently you jumped off a wall and broke your ankle, lol.

I appreciate everything you've done for me, from homemade cards to you giving me your Christmas bonus from your first job. Right from young, you always knew exactly what you did and didn't want. Do you remember that egg you didn't want to eat on holiday? So you lobbed it across the room in the restaurant, lol. You wanted to make a difference, be a mentor, a role model and you have done just that. I'm just sorry that I couldn't protect you from getting hurt over the years, from friends and family too. I still remember when you had your heart broken for the first time, mine broke for you.

You are amazing, you never give up, no matter what life throws at you. Remember that show you did at Jackie Palmer's? Your elastic broke on your trousers, you took them off, threw them across stage and carried on. The show must go on, that's what you said and that's what you have done. You are looked up to by so many of your subscribers and followers, but I am and always will be . . . your biggest fan.

Love, always,

   Mama

When I think of my sister, I always remember how much we used to fight! We'd argue over pretty much anything and I remember she punched me in my shoulder once, but I was too unwell to fight back so I laid in the hallway for a few hours and took a nap. At the time it probably wasn't that funny, but now it makes me laugh.

Over the years my relationship with Charlotte has grown and changed. Charlotte – or as everyone else calls her, Charleigh – is actually very different to me, despite how much we look alike. If I'm annoyed I cry, if she's annoyed she expresses anger, and trust me, that girl can be angry for weeks! She has always been a mummy's girl whereas I was and am independent, off doing my own thing.

But despite our differences I know we have each other's backs no matter what. She would be the first person to jump in and defend me if I ever needed it and vice versa. She is and always will be my sister. So when writing this book, I knew I wanted to include parts of our relationship, but I've struggled to express how I really feel. That's weird, isn't it? I've earned the title of the 'Internet's Big Sister', but in real life, the one person I *am* a big sister to is the person I find it hardest to give advice to, to be open with. I always wished I had an older sister growing up, so I don't want to miss this opportunity. For once, I am going to make myself say what I am thinking:

Charlotte, it probably hasn't been easy being my sister and it is not always easy being yours. We're stubborn (you a little more, lol), passionate and dynamic but we've been through a lot together. Some stuff you probably don't remember, but it was always just us and Mum. The Three Musketeers. The entire world will now know my story in full, but I also wish they could know yours. You've experienced childhood trauma, bullying, fuckboys (one too many) and crippling anxiety yet you still smile and laugh and continue to have a kind heart.

You're strong, SO strong, but you don't always have to be. I know at times you feel lost, like you should have your shit together, and I guess having a sister who (sort of) has adds even more pressure. But you're doing just fine so stop being so hard on yourself. The world is ready to give you everything you've ever dreamed of if you let it, if you would just trust yourself and the universe a little more. You can achieve everything you put your mind to – just don't give up.

You're beautiful. I love your outrageously big hair and your freckles – both of the things you used to dislike about yourself – I'm glad you love them just as much as I do now. You're funny, loyal and honest. You're shy but quietly confident and I'm slowly learning through therapy how wonderful it is to be your sister.

Enjoy life and have as much fun as you can. Stop being so angry and frustrated with people who don't really matter. Travel, try new food and take as many adventures as possible. Don't listen to your negative thoughts and turn every painful experience into something great.

Most of all thank you for loving me when I didn't believe I should be loved.

Final Thoughts

'Growing up with the childhood that I had, I learnt
to never let a man make me feel helpless. It also
embedded a deep need in me to stick up for women.'
Christina Aguilera

As I said at the beginning of this book: 'Trust your journey, as every point of your life is going to help you get to
where you need to be.' That has certainly been the case
with me. It feels like every single one of my life experiences has
made me who I am, and led up to this point in my life.

Of course there is a lot in my childhood that I would have
loved to have changed, but would I be where I am now if it hadn't
all happened the way it did? I doubt it. If I hadn't gone through
all that crap maybe I wouldn't have fought to get the kind of life
that as I lay in bed as a child I thought I could only dream of. More
importantly, I wouldn't be in a position to try and help others get
through the same, and live amazing lives.

The important thing is not to let your past define your future.
Even when I was in my deepest depression and completely

fucked, I knew that if I wanted to make a life for myself it depended on me and me alone. No one else could shape my world for me or carve out the path of my future. Where I needed to be and what was meant for me was down to me to achieve, so if I could just get up and get on with it, no one could take that from me.

You can't leave it all to destiny, you do need to put in the graft. I have always been really hard-working and given my all. Whether it was at dance lessons or taking on a difficult kid in the care home, I gave it everything, otherwise what is the point?

Passion and ambition, key things in life. I'm not sure my ambition will ever be satisfied. Maybe if I can afford to sail around the Caribbean on a yacht by the time I am sixty I will be tempted to relax, but even then …! My aim in life is to help women deal with social issues and taboos, and unfortunately I am sure they are not going to disappear in my lifetime, so my job will never be done. But when I die, I would like my legacy to be that I was part of a movement that helped change the way society views women's bodies and mental health.

I am hoping if you are reading this book that you are already part of that movement too, or are intending to be. We all deserve to be empowered, strong women who know how to love ourselves and those around us. I hope my story inspires you to go on your own discovery of self-love. Remember that no matter what you've been through, and no matter what people say about you, you *were* good enough, you *are* good enough, and you will *always* be good enough.

Ask Grace

R ight from the early days of the 'Ugly Face of Beauty', I have been contacted by people after advice or suggestions on how to deal with a situation.

Like I always say, I am no expert, but at the same time I know how to listen, have had training through the children's home, and have gone through many problems myself.

So as the 'Internet's Big Sister', I try to answer as many people as I can, honestly and openly. Where possible I'll do this on a public forum so that the individual can hopefully take something away from it, but also anyone else going through the same may benefit. Anything that makes people feel less isolated by their problems can only be a positive, right?

I asked you lovely people who follow me on Twitter and Instagram to send over any questions you may have and I have picked out eleven, trying to cover a range of topics.

Thanks for taking the time to get in touch, and hopefully my answers can be helpful in some way.

Questions

1) As a YouTuber, how do you stay confident when you're constantly under a microscope?

I am not sure I do allow myself to be constantly under the microscope. I always make sure I have time to myself, whether that is alone with my thoughts, relaxing with Simon, or chatting with friends. By having a sense of life away from social media, I feel like I protect myself to a degree. My YouTube life is an extension of my real life, not the other way around.

When I do go online and get negative comments I remind myself that those people don't know me the way I do, and if I like me, that is all that matters. I try and remember that often people who want to pick on how I look or the way I talk are cowards hiding behind their keyboards, suffering from jealousy or an unhappiness within themselves.

If things get really bad though, I come off the internet and talk to my friends to make sure I keep my self-confidence up. I never allow myself to get overly caught up in online hype, but try and stop any negative vibes from affecting my own energy.

I also avoid reading any press about myself, or the comments that follow on from it. Sometimes of course it is because I worry it will be negative and knock my confidence, but also I don't want to read positive pieces either, in case it goes to my head and I get an ego! I just want to keep grounded, humble and true to myself. I constantly tell myself I am here to create content, help people and live my life, and that's it.

2) Hi Gracie, what happens when you're in a relationship and the sex is just too vanilla? And no matter how many times you try to do something new, hint, beg (lol) . . . nothing changes? How can it progress without pushing your partner into something they don't want to do? Help me girl.

Hints or subtle comments, especially during sex, are not the way forward! They can ruin a moment, and cause resentment and misunderstanding. You need to sit and have an adult conversation with your partner when you are in a safe and relaxed environment away from the bedroom, say after dinner one evening. I am sure it will still be awkward, but if you really want to tackle things – and we all want to be enjoying the best sex life we can – you need to bite the bullet. Sex is a big part of every relationship so working on it is important.

I'd have to ask what the 'something new' is, though. If you are not climaxing for example and he is unwilling to try something that could change that, then yes, that is not fair, and he really needs to show willing.

But if it is just that you want to experiment with something a bit more out there and he is not comfortable with it, at the end of the day you need to respect his boundaries too.

It is all about being open with each other and willing to compromise and see what the other person needs from your sex life. At the end of the day you have to be able to sexually dance with each other, and your partner needs to know your song. Talking is really the only way to achieve that.

3) How do you 'practise what you preach'? I'm such a sup-porter of self-love no matter what your size, gender, race, sexuality – anything. You're beautiful no matter who you are. But I struggle applying this to the view I have of myself!

Aww, bless you, I understand that if you have spent years doing just about anything *but* love yourself, then it can be very hard to change your habits. Be kind to yourself and accept that it can be a gradual process to get there.

If you can't yet see yourself worthy of love, the technique I think works best is the one I describe in the self-care section, where you look at yourself in the third person, so see yourself as a child or a best friend. If you saw a close mate treated the way you treat yourself, maybe you wouldn't be too impressed, so you need to apply this thinking to yourself.

You owe it to your younger self – who it sounds like you may have neglected over the years – and to your own self now, to learn to look after yourself. Stop hating aspects of yourself that no one but you is judging you for, embrace all your positives, and slowly begin to love that person.

4) Hello, I'm a mum to two teenagers: a girl and a boy. My son is fourteen and bi. My daughter is seventeen and asex-ual. How do I make sure they're both secure and supported as they go through university and teenage years without smothering them? We have a good, open relationship but I want to make sure they're able to survive the crap they'll get for simply growing up, let alone anything else! Cx

Good on you for wanting to get this right! I think whatever sexuality your children identify as, the aim in raising them is the same. Every child should be so comfortable within themselves that if other people question who they are, it doesn't matter. You want them to be so secure in their own identity that no one can shake them from that.

I think honesty about how tough the world can be is necessary, along with positivity on how great it can be too.

You want them to be brave, resilient, courageous, and prepared for a world where people sadly aren't always nice. That doesn't have to be because you are bisexual or asexual, but because you are short, fat, black, whatever. At some point in life there is always someone who tries to make you a victim. So the important thing is to make your children strong enough that they don't fall prey to this.

It is good if they have support elsewhere, for example through the LGBT community and networks, and this can tide them over into university life. They need the space to develop and learn for themselves, so sometimes it is enough just to let them know you are there for them and will listen whenever they need, but then to stand back.

As they go on their journey to discover who they really are, just the knowledge alone that you are there and have their back is incredibly empowering for them.

5) What's the best way to heal yourself mentally/ emotionally?

Talking about the problem that has damaged you mentally or emotionally in the first place is the first step. Then you need to understand that recovering is a process that often includes grief, anger, tears and acceptance before you can get to where you want to be.

For me, talking though therapy is the key, so it's worth finding someone professional who can hold your trauma and baggage, and help you deal with your issues. Therapists have been trained to get you on the journey of healing, and can absolutely change your life. I know I wouldn't be where I am today without therapy.

Then you need to self-care, nurturing yourself the way you should be nurtured, and allowing yourself to heal. It takes time, and you need to give yourself that.

I'm also a big believer in music as an underrated form of therapy. Just one lyric can explain everything you are feeling and didn't know how to say, and certain tunes can act as an emotional release. We don't use it enough, but I do believe there is a song for every person, mood, feeling and issue, and it can be hugely helpful.

6) Hi Grace, what would be your advice to someone who has Generalised Anxiety Disorder who finds it hard to cope with confidence? And in rare moments of confidence what coping strategies would you recommend to prevent the anxiety from coming back as prominently as before?

I am sorry to hear you are going through this, but happy that you are looking for a way to try and move on from it.

My suggestion would be that the next time you are in a good place mentally, sit and write down a list of practical thoughts that your 'well mind' knows are facts. Include facts that will ring true regardless of the state you are in, such as 'I like jam on toast'. Then include facts that are true at that moment but can cause you anxiety in darker times, e.g., 'I have no problem getting the train on my own.'

Keep a copy of that list on your phone, in a notebook, by your bedside . . . anywhere you can easily access it if you need to. Then when you are in a state of anxiety you can look at it and remind yourself how your well mind thinks, and try to pull yourself into that same place.

Use the list to reassure and empower yourself. Trust it, and trust the well you. Accept the irrational thoughts you are having but don't listen to them; instead replace them with rational thoughts. Try to be very practical and factual with your mind, and hopefully over time the rational thoughts will begin to dominate. Best of luck.

7) How do you deal with toxic people that will always be in your life due to the fact they are relations?

I don't believe you have to keep anyone in your life if they really are toxic for you, relative or not. If they are not good for you, and repeatedly prove that, move away from them.

It is important to create your own world filled with people who make you feel good about yourself and uplift you, and for whom you do the same. For your own mental state it is important to clear toxic people out of your life. I have cut off family and friends for exactly that reason, as I value myself enough not to allow them into my space.

If you are still young though and unable to avoid certain situations at present, you need to put coping mechanisms in place. So prepare yourself when you are going to see the person, for example by writing lists of their positive points – even the shittiest person does have good traits. That way you can remind yourself of them throughout the event, party, meeting, whatever it is. Then afterwards if they have drained you or made you feel bad, make sure you cleanse the environment around you and look after yourself.

Remember that although toxic people aren't good for you, spending a small bit of time with them can teach you about resilience, how to be compassionate, and to be strong. If you can't escape spending time with them, then remember that in every toxic person or situation there is a lesson to be learnt.

8) Why do you think women talking about anything to do with sexual pleasure is a taboo?

Because sadly it is still a man's world! We are, however, moving in the right direction, and need to keep doing so. The position of women in society has been an issue since the dawn of time, but with each generation changes are happening, whether that is the ability to go out to work or vote.

Feminism and empowering women is so important, however you do it. I empower myself by not conforming to how I am told a woman should look, but instead learning to accept myself how I am, talking about women's issues and making sure sex is as enjoyable for me as the man.

Women and men are equal, but double standards are still an issue and it is important that people keep kicking back against them. Whether it is the media policing women's bodies, porn giving a ridiculous one-sided take on things, or companies thinking the ideal boss is a white man in a suit, too many societal norms are unfair and ridiculous.

But the more we talk about anything that is theoretically taboo, the more we can move things forwards and help heal society. Make sure you are part of the solution rather than the problem – get out there and proudly talk about female orgasms!

9) Hey. I'm twenty-one and starting to get on with my mum a lot more recently and would say we were friends, but I can't help thinking we're not connecting 100 per cent as she doesn't understand mental illness and feels that my anxiety does not exist. How can I talk to my mum to help her understand a bit more?

The way our parents were brought up was very different to us, so accepting that her not understanding mental illness is a lack of knowledge rather than her not loving or caring for you is a good starting point. I am sure she will support you through it once she has a better grasp on it.

So if I were you I would try to educate her, by showing her videos, articles and books, and maybe even taking her along to the doctor with you and getting them to explain what you are going through, whether that is anxiety, depression or whatever. Sometimes hearing it from a person who is an authority on the topic can help a parent to accept its seriousness.

If you aren't comfortable bringing up the topic initially, a good way to communicate something important to a parent can be through a letter. It lets them know you want to talk about how you feel and to lay out the facts and your emotions for them to think about in their own time.

When it came to me telling Mum about the sexual abuse I describe earlier in the book, I actually wrote that to her in a text as I just didn't know how to say the words. It allowed her to process it, and then we followed that up with a long conversation. It worked well for both of us.

10) Do you have any advice on dealing with extremely low self-esteem (particularly body image) in relation to sex and relationships?

I would say if a boy has got to the stage where he wants to have sex with you, he will already have a pretty good idea of what your body looks like. They can see your shape and type through your clothes, and wow, look at that, he still wants to have sex with you! Trust that a boy knows what you look like, would like to be with you, and take that for the compliment that it is.

Then once you are in the moment, I promise you the last thing they care about is whether you have any so-called flaws on your body. I have honestly never met a guy who gives a fuck about cellulite or stretchmarks, especially in the midst of sex, or going into a relationship. Your body isn't supposed to look a certain way, no matter what society, the media or other people may say.

On the off-chance you are ever unlucky enough to come across a guy who does judge your body in any way, don't you dare have sex with him, but get right out of there. He doesn't deserve you, so make sure you find someone who does.

Remind yourself that your body is literally a vessel for the person inside you, and that is the part of you that matters. Our bodies aren't supposed to be perfect. Any boy worth being with will know that too.

Then focus on actually enjoying the sex, think about the pleasure of the feelings rather than what everything looks like.

11) How have you changed since becoming a figure in the public eye regarding body image? What I mean is, are you more critical of yourself, because thousands of people view you, or have you gone the opposite way and thought f* you? I hope that makes some sense** ☺

Good question! I think I am less critical of myself. After I found the body positive community I learnt to replace the negative thoughts with positive ones, so it is like I have reprogrammed my brain. The negative thoughts will still appear, but now each one is just a thought that I acknowledge, but refuse to follow through with. They become like the other thoughts in life that you already know how to process. For example, I am walking down the street, a guy spits on the floor, it's disgusting and I have a thought that I'd love to slap him! But of course I don't, it is a gut emotional reaction, but one I will never actually act on. It is the same now if I have a negative thought that I look ugly and want to self-harm as a result. Now it is just a thought that I don't act out. I acknowledge the feeling is there, but I don't pander to it.

Of course I still have down days, everyone does – even Beyoncé, I am sure, sometimes hates her body or the way she looks. But I now accept that happens and that is when I practise more self-care and work even harder to love myself, and then I get through it, even if sometimes I don't know how I am going to.

After spending so many of my younger years consumed by trying to be someone I was not, now I am working on the real me. Trying to be someone else didn't work, and I couldn't love myself while I was doing it, but now I have accepted me for me, I can.

Acknowledgements

Bringing this book to life has been both cathartic and draining, but it's also been such an incredible opportunity that I still can't believe it is actually happening. What is my life like? Lol! I definitely keep pinching myself because it's all so surreal.

The biggest thank you goes to my team who have been with me for the past three years and have helped to elevate my career to a level I had only ever dreamed of. Andy, Katie, Rosa, Hana, Becky and my babe of a manager James – you make my life so much easier (and busier!) and I would be lost without you.

To everyone who played a part in allowing me to tell my story: To my agent James Wills at Watson Little and to Emma Donnan who helped me get this crazy life of mine down on the pages, your support and belief has been tremendous. Sarah, Grace, Frances and Vicky from Headline – you have been a pleasure to work with. I love you all so much!

A massive thank you to my loved ones, whether you have been with me my entire life or just a few short months. Thank you for allowing me to be myself and loving me through it all – especially the hard times. When I think back there are a few names that pop up time and time again:

Laren – you are my oldest friend and I wish SO much that I could see you more. Thank you for sticking with me for so long. I love you.

Miss 'Mary' McCrystal – my favourite teacher at school who made me feel safe and wanted and that I was capable of anything. I wish every child had a chance to be taught by you.

Michelle – thank you for teaching me the importance of a good childhood and allowing me into your home pretty much whenever. You, Jessica and Wiggy are like my family. Miss you always!

Jay and Jade – although things aren't how they used to be, thank you for showing me what a healthy relationship looks like. You gave me the starting point in knowing what I wanted to do with my life and for that, I'm truly thankful.

Tom – my singing teacher who told me at 12 'one day you'll be a star'. Your words have stayed with me forever. Thanks for believing in me when I was struggling to believe in myself.

Callie, Danie, Lottie, Chloe, Beth, Vix – I LOVE YOU!!!!!!! At some point in my life you have all been there for me when I needed you the most. Thank you for keeping me grounded and coming on this journey with me.

Nai, Steph and Erica – you are my home. I never want to live in a world without you.

My spiritual family at The Recover Clinic, to whom I owe my life. Emmy, you saved me and I will never be able to repay you. You were the light that I needed at the darkest time and you made me understand myself in a way that I didn't know was possible. You are far too pure for this world and I thank my lucky stars every day that you came into my life. Please, never change.

An enormous thank you to my Mum and sister Charleigh – you are all I've ever known and the memories we have together will stay with me for the rest of my life. It hasn't been easy has it? But my God has it been worth it. I hope you're proud of me. There are no words to express how much I love you both.

Simon – thank you for allowing me to fuck up, to get lost, to grow and then to find myself. I love you! x

My subscribers, my followers, my friends on the internet thank you in abundance for all of your encouragement, understanding and support. None of this would be possible without all that you do for me. What a journey it's been hey?

And lastly thank you to my younger self for being strong, resilient and a total fighter. Without you, I wouldn't be the woman I am today. You set the foundations for the amazing life I lead now and I am everything I am because of you. We made it girl … we got a fucking book!